The Thames

A History from the Air

Leslie Banks and Christopher Stanley

Oxford   New York

OXFORD UNIVERSITY PRESS

1990

Oxford University Press, Walton Street, Oxford OX2 6DP

Oxford New York Toronto
Delhi Bombay Calcutta Madras Karachi
Petaling Jaya Singapore Hong Kong Tokyo
Nairobi Dar es Salaam Cape Town
Melbourne Auckland
and associated companies in
Berlin Ibadan

Oxford is a trade mark of Oxford University Press

British Library Cataloguing in Publication Data
Banks, Leslie
The Thames : a history from the air.
1. England. Thames River, history
I. Title. II. Stanley, Christopher
942.2
ISBN 0–19–215895–3

Library of Congress Cataloging in Publication Data
Banks, Leslie.
The Thames : a history from the air / Leslie Banks and Christopher Stanley.
p.   cm.
1. Thames River (England)—Aerial photographs. 2. Thames River
(England)—History—Pictorial works. 3. Thames River (England)—Description and
travel—Views. 4. Historic sites—England—Thames River Valley—Pictorial works.
I. Stanley, Christopher. II. Title.
914.22'0022'2—dc20 DA670.T2B27 1990 89–78182
ISBN 0–19–215895–3

Typeset by Latimer Trend & Co. Ltd
Printed in Hong Kong

*T*HE Thames is a great river. It is not the longest river in Britain (that honour belongs to the Severn), but it is without doubt our most important. Its position in the south of England, an area pivotal to British history, pointing eastwards to the continent of Europe as a funnel inviting invaders and settlers, has cast the river in a special historic role.

According to present wisdom, the source is a series of streams draining south from the Cotswold slopes, and maps show Thameshead to be at Trewsbury Mead, some three miles west of Cirencester. The eastern extent of the river is open to interpretation. Where does the funnel of the estuary become the North Sea? For this book we have looked at the historical aspects of the river in a geographical setting extending from Shoeburyness in the north to Sheerness in the south ('ness' is from the Old English, a 'nose' cutting off the sea), with one or two excursions to comment on some special historical attractions on the north-east coast of Kent.

This study is a history of the River Thames and the Thames basin, illustrated by aerial photographs taken over the last fifteen years. The photographs were not taken with a sophisticated aerial device, but with an ordinary 35 mm SLR camera. We flew in Cessna 172 and Grumman AA5 aircraft based at Denham airfield in Buckinghamshire. Our technique was to fly along the river at heights ranging from 500 to 1,500 feet, depending on the location and the degree of detail we wished to include in the picture. The flights were carried out in all seasons because the opportunities for aerial photography in the Thames Valley are limited. To take really clear photographs, free from haze, a horizontal visibility in excess of 30 miles is required—even if the target is only a few hundred yards away, for it is essential to be able to capture close detail. Excellent visibility is not a characteristic of the Thames Valley: it can occur in freshly washed air behind a showery airstream, but on frustratingly few occasions in each year. We searched ahead and planned our approach in terms of both height and angle, taking into consideration the target size, its position in relation to background features essential for proper identification, wind drift,

Preface

lighting level in relation to cloud and sun, and the direction of the sun in order to minimize the effects of any persisting haze. For certain subjects and lighting conditions, the challenge of producing good pictures requires a high degree of co-ordination between pilot and photographer. The aircraft, initially approaching along a calculated line, might have to be tilted to enter a spiral over the target, at which point the photographer can lean out of the plane to take the photographs.

The pictures we have selected for this book, from among the thousands we have taken over the years, are intended to illustrate the essential partnership of Man and River, from earliest times up to the present day. We hope the reader will derive as much pleasure from examining this record as we have enjoyed in its compilation.

Acknowledgements

*T*HE interpretation of history in this book draws its material and inspiration from many sources. Relevant facts on geology and geography have been provided by the libraries of the Institute of Geological Sciences and the Royal Geographical Society, and we have drawn on the expertise of the Remote Sensing Centre at Farnborough. For ancient history we must thank the Berkshire Archaeological Society and the Middle Thames Archaeological and Historical Society, and the Ashmolean Museum at Oxford, which is the keeper of the pioneer photographic work of O. G. S. Crawford and Major G. W. Allen. Our knowledge of the middle periods of history has benefited from many publications, including those of the National Trust and the Maritime Trust, and from personal contact with Brigadier J. Hamilton-Baillie, MC, and the late Bill Gardam of the Thames Society. For information on various aspects of the modern Thames environment, we are indebted to the Central Electricity Generating Board, the Thames Water Authority, the London Borough of Barking and Dagenham, and the Ramblers' Association. Finally, special thanks to our colleague Mrs Edna Goodburn for her contributions to this enterprise over a number of years. Her assistance in the air, and on the ground in the marshalling of historical data, has been invaluable.

Contents

Illustrations

Chapter 7
Enjoying the River

Other Illustrations

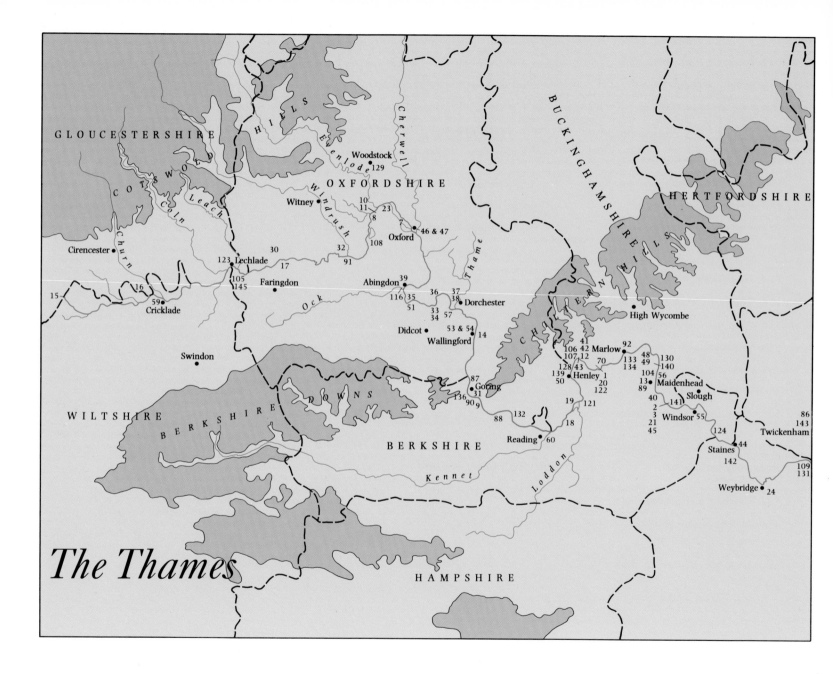

GLOUCESTERSHIRE

COTSWOLD HILLS

Coln

Leach

Churn

Cirencester

Witney

OXFORDSHIRE

Woodstock • 129

Evenlode

Cherwell

Windrush

10
11   23
8

Oxford • 46 & 47

108

Thame

HERTFORDSHIRE

BUCKINGHAMSHIRE

30

32

91

123 Lechlade

17

105
145

Faringdon

15

16

59
Cricklade

Ock

Abingdon 39

116 35 36   37
51   38 57
      33 34

Didcot

53 & 54
Wallingford 14

Dorchester

High Wycombe

Swindon

WILTSHIRE

BERKSHIRE DOWNS

87
136 Goring
31
90 9

88   132

19   121

18

Reading • 60

Kennet

CHILTERN HILLS

41
106 42 Marlow 92
107 12   70   48 130
128 43   133 49 140
139   134 104 56
50 Henley 1   13
      20   89 Maidenhead
      122   Slough
                  40
                  2   141
                  3   Windsor 55
                  21   124
                  45

Loddon

BERKSHIRE

HAMPSHIRE

The Thames

86
143
Twickenham

Staines 44
142

109
131

Weybridge • 24

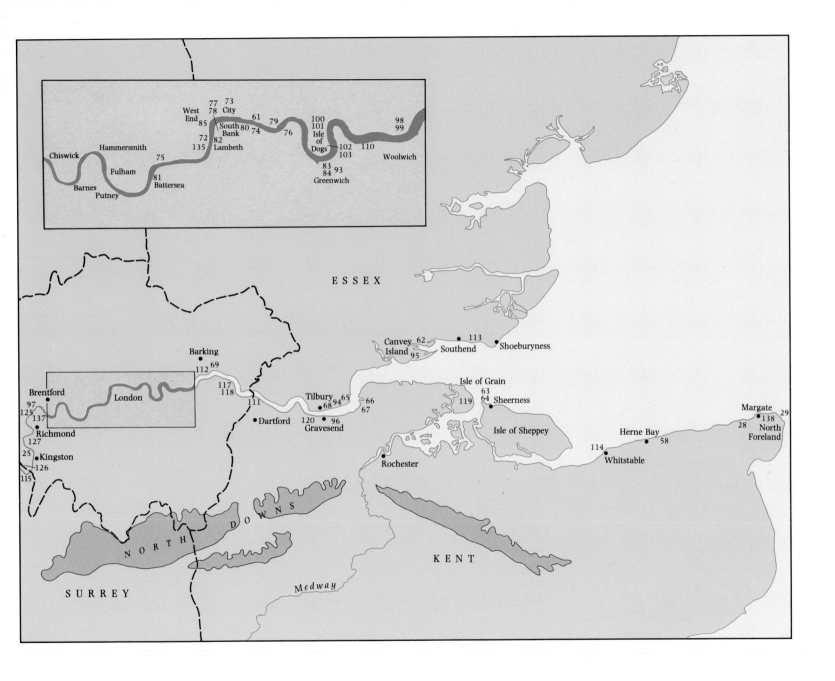

West End
77 73
78 City
85
61 79
South 80
Bank 74 76
72
82
135 Lambeth
Chiswick
Hammersmith
Fulham
75
81
Barnes Battersea
Putney

100
101 Isle
of
Dogs
102
103 110
83 93
84
Greenwich

98
99
Woolwich

ESSEX

Barking
112 69
117
118
111

Canvey 62
Island 113
95 Southend
Shoeburyness

Isle of Grain
63
119 64 Sheerness

Tilbury 65
68 94 66
67

Brentford
97
London
125
137
Richmond
127
25
Kingston
126
115

Dartford

120 96
Gravesend

Isle of Sheppey

Margate
28 North
Foreland
138 29

Herne Bay
58
114
Whitstable

Rochester

NORTH DOWNS

KENT

SURREY

Medway

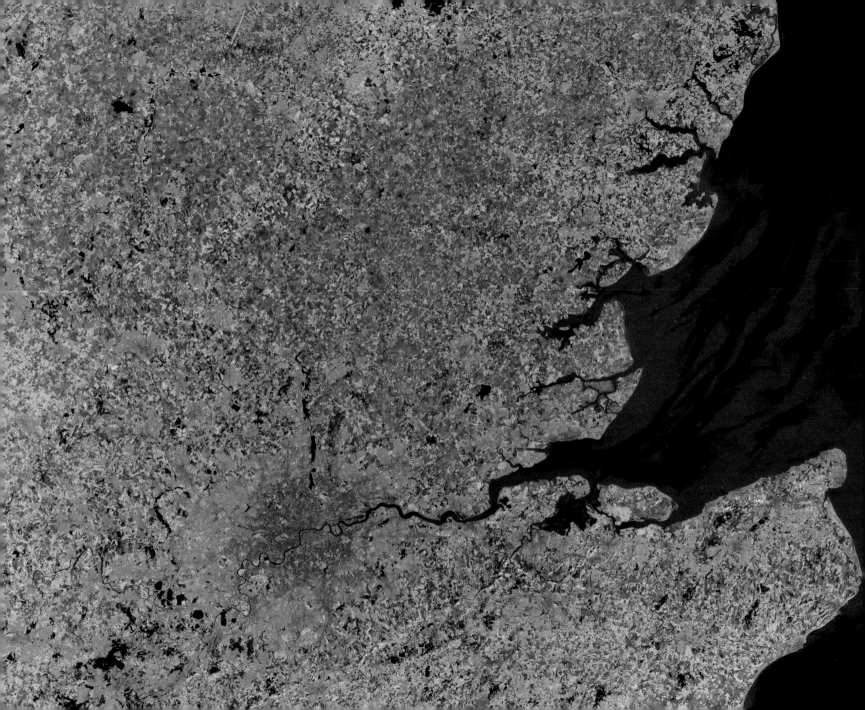

Landsat image

Low-level aerial photography
produces impressive local detail,
but is inevitably subject to the
whim of the English weather.
Satellite images provide
information on large-scale
structures, and if infra-red
cameras are used they can more
readily penetrate the dust and
moisture haze below them. The
images are, of course, transmitted
to ground stations by radio, and
detail missed on one pass can be
captured on a later pass and
integrated into the electronically
recorded image of the territory.
Interpretation of these images is
based on the arbitrary selection of
'false colour' responses to the
non-optical frequencies recorded
by the system. Illustrated here is
the selection of blue for towns, red
for agricultural land, and black for
water, in a Landsat image
covering the Thames estuary as
far as Sheerness and
Shoeburyness, and west of London
out to Heathrow airport, which is
clearly visible. Further west,
unfortunately, the Thames cannot
easily be picked out at this scale.

Reproduced by permission of the
Royal Aerospace Establishment,
Farnborough.

The Thames
A History from the Air

THE RIVER'S TALE

Twenty bridges from Tower to Kew—
(Twenty bridges or twenty-two)—
Wanted to know what the River knew,
For they were young and the Thames was old,
And this is the tale that the River told :—

I walk my beat before London Town,
Five hours up and seven down.
Up I go till I end my run
At Tide-end-town, which is Teddington.
Down I come with the mud in my hands
And plaster it over the Maplin Sands.
But I'd have you know that these waters of mine
Were once a branch of the River Rhine,
When hundreds of miles to the East I went
And England was joined to the Continent.

I remember the bat-winged lizard-birds,
The Age of Ice and the mammoth herds,
And the giant tigers that stalked them down
Through Regent's Park into Camden Town.
And I remember like yesterday
The earliest Cockney who came my way,
When he pushed through the forest that lined the Strand,
With paint on his face and a club in his hand.

He was death to feather and fin and fur.
He trapped my beavers at Westminster.
He netted my salmon, he hunted my deer,
He killed my heron off Lambeth Pier.
He fought his neighbour with axes and swords,
Flint or bronze, at my upper fords,
While down at Greenwich, for slaves and tin,
The tall Phoenician ships stole in,
And North Sea war-boats, painted and gay,
Flashed like dragon-flies, Erith way;
And Norseman and Negro and Gaul and Greek
Drank with the Britons in Barking Creek,

And life was gay, and the world was new,
And I was a mile across at Kew!
But the Roman came with a heavy hand,
And bridged and roaded and ruled the land,
And the Roman left and the Danes blew in—
And that's where your history-books begin!

RUDYARD KIPLING

W'HY does distant observation lend the
archaeologist special powers? O. G. S. Crawford,
who more than anybody else put aerial
archaeology on the map, drew a comparison between the
view of an oriental carpet as seen by a cat and a person
standing above it. The 'cat's eye view' cannot reveal the
broad pattern of the loom.

Originally conceived as an adjunct to ground work and
excavation, aerial archaeology has now become an
independent instrument for discovery. The photographic
record is more than a map, it is a compendium of
evidence for interpretation by the archaeologist and the
historian. The slightest unevenness or disturbance of the
ground's surface can be shown; totally buried sites, given
favourable circumstances, will be strikingly revealed. It is
possible for a series of overlapping cultures to be seen in a
single picture, say a neolithic *cursus* (pathway), overlaid
successively by a Bronze Age camp, a Roman villa, and a
derelict medieval village overtaken by the plague.

It is recorded that the idea of studying archaeology by
means of air photography occurred to a balloonist in the
late nineteenth century. The first photography carried out
from an aeroplane is said to have been done by L. P.
Bonvillain in 1908, in an aircraft flown by Wilbur
Wright, and during the First World War aerial
photography became a standard reconnaissance
technique. After the war, O. G. S. Crawford, who had
flown as a front-line cameraman, set about the
pioneering task of developing the technique of aerial
archaeology.

Chapter 1

Aerial Archaeology

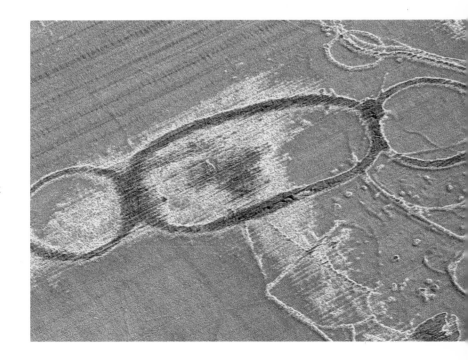

Crawford's investigations were mainly conducted above the chalklands of Wessex, which are both rich in archaeological remains and have conditions suitable for revealing them. Another area with the right mixture for successful research is the upper Thames Valley, and Major G. W. Allen, Crawford's successor as an aerial photographer, completely revolutionized archaeology in that region. Using a home-made camera (now in the archives of the Ashmolean Museum at Oxford), and flying in all seasons, Allen discovered many hitherto unknown sites. From 1933 to 1939, Allen made a systematic search of southern England, and gathered a body of information which is the basis of our understanding of the technique of aerial archaeology. His headquarters were at Oxford, and his historic photographs, taken mainly from a height of 1,000–1,500 feet, are still on view at the Ashmolean. Allen wrote the following about his work: 'The signs are there for all to see; nor is there anything magical or mysterious about them. Nevertheless, there is a thrill in seeing and re-discovering these long-lost evidences of human endeavour.'

As noted by Allen, there are five different kinds of marks to be observed from the air.

1. Shadows thrown by banks and mounds only slightly raised above the general ground level. They are most visible when the sun is low on the horizon. (Plate 4.)

2. Snow and frost marks caused by the more rapid melting of snow or hoar-frost over areas that have been excavated and refilled, or where there are actual structures beneath the surface. Snow may also reveal surface inequalities since drifting can produce patterns similar to those of shadow sites. (Plate 6.)

3. Floods covering low-lying ground may reveal patterns by leaving significant areas unsubmerged, again with effects similar to those of shadow sites.

4. Soil marks, which occur when some disturbance, such as the digging of a ditch or the raising of a bank, has caused an alteration in the content of the surface soil. The effect is quite striking when surface humus is underlaid with chalk. Damp marks, on the other hand, become visible through differences in humidity. Ditches which have been filled with silt and humus act as sponges, retaining moisture longer than the surrounding soil. Such ditches show dark against their drier background (Plate 5). In practice these marks are usually confined to the winter and early spring, and are common in periods of drought. At other times the moisture effects are usually masked by growing crops, but then the site will often show crop marks.

5. Crop marks are caused by disturbances of the soil which affect the growth of a crop. Generally the marks are due to more luxuriant growth, richer colour, or greater height of the crop; but earlier germination, partial failure, or weaker growth can also give useful results. For a crop mark to appear, there must in the past have been some alteration of the surface affecting the depth or richness of the topsoil, so that the crops growing over that disturbed area have some reason to differ from those

in the rest of the field. Crop marks can appear above filled-in ditches, flattened earthworks, or the buried walls of buildings.

Stinging nettles grow profusely in areas of rich soil which have been disturbed, and their presence is an indicator of the ditches surrounding ancient settlements. Ring ditches occur on the gravel terraces along both banks of the Thames, from Cirencester down to Goring, but are extremely rare (the authors, like Allen, have found none) in the lower Thames Valley. Usually the rings appear close to the river, and they generally occur in groups; however, isolated rings have been observed in circumstances where it is unlikely that others of an associated group would have been missed. It often happens that these circles are cut by other marks of a different period.

Disturbances of the ground can enrich the surface soil, and lead to the early blossoming of certain plants. Rape and poppy may produce vivid yellow and red marks against a background of grass or crop, the poppies of Flanders providing the classic example. Sometimes crop marks are visible simultaneously in grass, barley, wheat, and oats. Those in barley are generally the most pronounced, while differences in growth in oats are least evident. Growth differentials are attributed mainly to differences in the root length of the crop.

It is rare for crop marks to appear in profusion over a wide area, and there are some years when no significant crop marks have appeared at all. Some may show up only once in a lifetime. An example is the ploughed-out burial circles of the Bronze Age at Crowmarsh, North Stoke, in Oxfordshire. Our photograph (Plate 14) was taken in 1976: the marks were visible for only three days, and have never shown up with such clear definition since then.

Crop marks arising from growth enhancement are known as positive crop marks. In a field of cereal these show as a darker green while the crop is growing, and later, during ripening, as greener lines in a field which is turning yellow. Plants producing the over-luxuriant growth of a positive crop mark can also collapse in bad weather.

Growth reduction, and early parching in a summer stand of crop, produce negative crop marks. These occur, for example, when soil depth is reduced by a buried road or other obstruction to root penetration, and channels are seen in the crop reflecting the obstructions below, or there is a yellowing of the affected crop early in the harvesting period. To illustrate both positive and negative marks, a photograph is reproduced taken by Allen at ground level of a crop mark at Burcot, near Dorchester in Oxfordshire. A gravel pit had cut into a field of standing corn, revealing a filled-in ditch beneath a positive mark, and a buried structure beneath a negative mark.

Unfortunately soil and crop marks represent a stage in the destruction of early remains by the plough. The mixing of the soil by repeated cultivation causes the marks to become less distinct with every ploughing cycle. However, if deeper ploughing brings fresh material to the surface (and modern ploughs reach about 9 inches deeper than their predecessors), the marks are regenerated. The very processes of agriculture which were responsible for the obliteration of sites are now, thanks to aerial photography, instrumental in their discovery. One of the most striking results of recent aerial work has been the discovery of sites along the Thames in an area which was previously devoid of crop marks, and which had been believed to be unsuitable for early settlement. A major factor seems to be the ploughing of once-permanent pasture.

Official steps have been taken to preserve the records of such discoveries, exemplified by the establishment of the Cambridge University Collection and the Curatorship in Aerial Photography. The Royal Commission on Historic Monuments aims to complete a detailed archaeological map of this country, based on aerial photography, in 1992. The map will show several hundred thousand sites,

of which 25 per cent are likely to be prehistoric, 25 per cent Romano-British, and 50 per cent medieval. It will be the most comprehensive operation of its kind in the world. The value of aerial work has been demonstrated by its survey of the middle and upper Thames Valley, which has revealed many new sites, including one at Stadhampton in Oxfordshire. The Stadhampton site lies only two miles from Dorchester-on-Thames, at the heart of one of the most intensively surveyed areas of England. Despite half a century of unbroken aerial surveillance, no trace of this important find had been seen before.

Burcot Pit Reproduced by kind permission of the Ashmolean Museum, this photograph shows a transection of Burcot Pit, Oxfordshire. Quarrying has conveniently produced the evidence underlying the crop marks in a field of oats. The areas of enhanced and reduced growth are clearly identified: a former ditch has encouraged the accumulation of vegetable matter leading to nutritional enrichment, and a buried structure has restricted the supply of water or nutrients to the overlying crop.

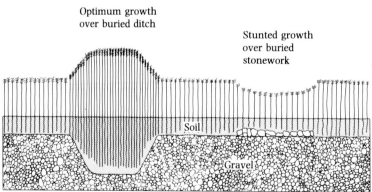

Optimum growth
over buried ditch

Stunted growth
over buried
stonework

Soil

Gravel

1. Medmenham, Bucks.

The people cruising down the Thames cannot see the evidence of the history lying hidden on the river bank behind them. The evidence is reserved for the aerial view. On a slight slope overlooking the river there is a single circle, the remains of a Bronze Age round barrow showing up as a darker green in a ripening crop of wheat.

2 & 3. Iron Age Farmstead, Dorney, and Butser Hill

The farmstead at Dorney in Buckinghamshire is buried almost six feet below the present ground level, and is revealed by changes in both the height and the colour of a ripening crop of barley. The site is located some 300 feet from the present bank of the Thames, and at certain times of the year would probably have become waterlogged and muddy underfoot. A layer of flint stones was therefore laid and compacted over the ground surface, which has resulted in the lighter colour of the crop. When the site was in use it would have been very similar to the modern reconstruction of an Iron Age farmstead at Butser Hill in Hampshire, which is shown alongside for comparison.

For many years it was assumed that the people of the Iron Age lived mostly within the confines of their hill-forts, but aerial photography has changed our perception of life in that period. We now know that they normally lived on farms, and only took refuge in hill-forts in times of emergency.

7

4. Shadow marks, Oxon.

Here, in an unploughed area, the boundaries of ancient fields are clearly identified in shadow relief by the evening sun. A similar effect is the way road undulations show up in car headlights at night. Compare this picture with the field patterns in Plate 5.

5. Soil marks, Oxon. Downs

The Oxfordshire Downs between
the Thames and the Ridgeway.
The outlines of ancient fields show
up as colour differences in a
recently ploughed field.

6. Snow marks on the Ridgeway, Oxon.

This photograph was taken when the river banks had a light dusting of snow. The group of diagonal lines running from top right to bottom left of the picture is the Ridgeway, which is one of the oldest trackways in England, dating from the prehistoric period. Although for much of its course the route is well defined, the point where it crosses the Thames to join the Icknield Way has been a matter of considerable speculation. It very rarely becomes visible except under conditions like those in the picture, when a light covering of snow has been subject to drifting, revealing irregularities of the ground surface.

7. Binsey, Oxon.

An interesting example of how many periods of history can show up as
crop marks on the same site. The parallel lines are the ploughed-out
remains of a medieval ridge and furrow cultivation system. The other
marks, circles and polygons, are believed to date from the Iron Age
through to the Roman, and possibly even the Saxon period. The River
Thames is just visible in the top left corner of the picture.

8. Foxley Farm, Eynsham, Oxon.

An excellent example of crop marks in an area of abundant archaeological sites. The intense green coloration of the affected plants reveals various forms of enclosure, indicating devices to define territory or constrain livestock. Accumulation of humus at these boundaries has encouraged growth of the crop. We can also see the positive crop marks of trackways. The very prominent circles, and the ellipse with rounded extensions, are believed to date from the late Stone Age, but there are indications of continuing occupation up to the Roman period.

9. Lower Basildon, Berks.

A most unusual crop mark, caused by the early flowering of a crop of rape above the buried remains of a Roman villa and associated features in its grounds. This precocity does not come about every year. The first indications of a Roman site were found during the ground preparations for the railway track running across the picture.

13

10 & 11. Foxley Farm, Eynsham

The area around Eynsham in Oxfordshire contains one of the densest sets of crop marks in southern England. Though relatively sparsely populated today with scattered houses and farms, this area saw great human activity in prehistoric times. There are no indications of the extent of early settlement visible at ground level, and very few ancient artefacts have been recovered from the soil. Indeed, but for the development of aerial archaeology, very little would be known about the early settlement of this area. The first picture shows an elongated enclosure (perhaps the remains of a prehistoric long barrow) with two circles, one at each end. If the picture is compared with the second one, taken ten years later, the variation in the crop marks can be seen. The second picture shows details which were not visible ten years earlier. It is important to fly over sites a number of times in order to develop a complete picture of the crop mark record. In some years, depending on weather patterns, the nature of the crop, and farming practice, there may be no yield of crop marks, while the succeeding year may show them in abundance and in detail never suspected.

12. Mill End, Bucks.

In the centre of the photograph, close to the river, is the outline of a large Roman villa. The image is produced when the grass lying above the wall foundations is parched. Normally grass does not show crop marks except in conditions of extreme dry weather. This photograph was taken during a period of drought in June 1989. The size of the villa may be judged from the scale of the modern houses in the village.

13. Ray Mead, Maidenhead, Berks.

The curving stream in the right of the picture is White Brook, which enters the Thames close to Boulter's Lock, near Maidenhead. The field adjacent to the stream contains four circles which are the ploughed-out remains of Bronze Age barrows showing up in a ripening crop of barley. Also shown are surface indications of the ditches, now buried well underground, which once surrounded the burial mounds. At the bottom left of the picture there is a faint rectangular trace of an ancient feature, possibly a building or an animal enclosure.

14. Crowmarsh, North Stoke, Oxon.

This field contains the crop marks of many Bronze Age burial mounds, all trace of which has completely disappeared at ground level. Many such sites situated alongside the Thames have been continuously ploughed for centuries because of the fertility of the soil. Photographed in midsummer, when the wheat crop is in the process of ripening, the outlines of the moisture-laden, nutrient-rich ditches which once surrounded the barrows are clearly visible as areas where the crop has continued feeding and delayed its ripening.

Chapter 2

The Natural Setting for Development

THE landscape of Britain possesses an extraordinary variety of geological formations. The north and west of our island group shows surface rocks of diverse geological histories, overlaid and mixed in complex patterns. In the south and east, the rocks are generally overlaid with strata originating from biological or alluvial deposits. It is difficult to be certain about the ancient history of the earth, and our views may be modified by the availability of satellite imagery, which has already revealed the presence of hitherto unsuspected structural features.

The significant outcrop in the low-lying Thames Valley region is a chalk escarpment extending through Wiltshire, Oxfordshire, Berkshire, and Buckinghamshire. The general chalk layer forming the escarpment was deposited from the extensive (but shallow) chalk sea that existed over 100 million years ago, in the cretaceous period. The Thames cuts through this escarpment at the Goring Gap, north and east of which lie the Chiltern Hills. To the west, beyond the chalk ridge, there is a succession of valleys formed from clays, and ridges formed from limestones and sandstones. The remainder of the region comprises the middle of the London basin, an area covered by rocks newer than the chalk. Essex, an alluvial plain cut by numerous rivers, slopes gently down to the North Sea and the Thames estuary. Along the river and its estuary there are strips of silt, edged by gravel terraces.

The Thames was once confluent with the Rhine, both rivers debouching into the lowland basin which later became the North Sea. For two million years, up to about

ten thousand years ago, Britain suffered a regime of changing climate popularly known as the ice-ages. The evidence of man's early development spans this period. The last 10,000-year span of geological history is known as the holocene (recent) period, during which the massive ice sheet extending from Scandinavia to Britain, which had engulfed all but the south of England, slowly receded. It never encroached significantly on the Thames Valley area as we know it today, though in winter glacial marks, resembling damp marks but over glacial moraines, can sometimes be seen in the bare soil of cultivated fields. In Britain, man enjoyed an early start in the relatively ice-free area of the Thames Valley. However, a bitter periglacial climate prevailed, only becoming milder with the thinning of the ice. This thinning was accompanied by the widespread tilting of the land, relieved of the weight of ice in the north, which led to the separation of Britain from the Continent.

Before the glaciations, the lower reaches of the Thames lay further north than today. From Marlow the old course went through Rickmansworth, the Vale of St Albans, and Hertford, presumably escaping to its confluence with the Rhine. The present Blackwater River probably marks this early path of the Thames. The river moved to its present course in three stages. During the first period, the ice extended southwards to deposit debris in the Vale of St Albans, and the obstructed Thames escaped south-east along the Finchley Depression to rejoin its former course near Ware. Secondly, advancing ice from the Lowestoft ice sheet blocked both the Vale of St Albans and the

Finchley Depression: the Thames then diverted into its present basin, but north of its present course. In the third stage, when the ice finally retreated it left glacial deposits, so that the former Thames valley was still blocked, and the Thames moved south within its basin to reach its present course, leaving terraces to mark the heights of its former levels.

In the period from 8000 BC (the beginning of the holocene) to 3500 BC, man lived in communities of hunters. The oscillations of temperature were quite exceptional during this relatively short time-span, and the play of the weather provided a range of conditions in which many species lived and developed. By the time of the appearance of Thames Valley settlers in quantity (4,000 to 6,000 years ago), there had grown up huge virgin forests of oak, ash, and beech. The natural vegetation of the area was now complete, but early man was to start on the forests' destruction, and of course few of them survive today.

15. The source of the Thames, Glos.

The wooded area in the centre of the picture, one mile south-west of Trewsbury House, near Thameshead, is claimed to be the source of the River Thames and is marked on maps as such. Current wisdom recognizes that no single trickling stream can be deemed the source of a great river. In the case of the Thames, a number of local springs feed the river, which is joined by many tributaries on its path to the sea.

16. South Cerney, Glos.

This area, not far from the supposed source of the Thames, is covered by
oolitic limestone gravels which were laid down by the action of the river
as it cut its way through the valley in former times. Today these gravels
supply material used in the manufacture of concrete, and the large
extraction pits have become filled with water. The considerable changes
in the landscape are clearly shown in this photograph.

17. The upper Thames, east of Radcot Lock

Between Rushey Lock and Radcot Lock the river meanders through the Oxfordshire countryside. The terraces beside the river are changing from flint gravel to the oolitic limestone of the Cotswold Hills. The river banks in this area sometimes reveal crop marks, but when this photograph was taken, in June of 1988 (normally the height of the crop mark season), the relatively wet summer produced a lush green landscape without any traces of earlier habitation.

18. The Thames in winter, Sonning

A view of the Thames in winter livery, showing the island Hallsmead Eyot near Sonning, Berkshire. The countryside is covered with a mantle of snow and the river shows in black contrast.

19. The Thames at Shiplake →

The river flows gently across its flood-plain towards the town of Reading, which can be seen in the background of the picture. The river terrace has been quarried extensively for gravel in recent years, although the area shown here is relatively untouched due to pressure from conservationists. In the gravel pits nearby there have been discovered ancient artefacts including stone axes dating from a quarter of a million years ago. Some of the discoveries are on view in Reading Museum.

20. Meandering to Medmenham

In its path from source to estuary the Thames passes through only one significant hill, the chalk escarpment of the Chiltern–Berkshire range, which is broken at the Goring Gap. At Medmenham in Buckinghamshire, ten miles east of the Goring Gap, the river has actually travelled over 15 miles in its weaving path from Goring, passing through Pangbourne and Reading.

21. Dorney, Bucks.

The river has changed its course several times in the past, significantly when influenced by ice-age encroachments and floods of melt water seeking new channels. The present course of the Thames can be seen on the right of the picture, but the ripening corn on the left contains some darker patches which delineate former channels. The banks of those earlier channels were populated in prehistory, particularly in the Bronze and Iron Ages, and many artefacts have been recovered in the area. This picture is a good example of the use of aerial photography in the understanding of geography. The old river channels are clearly marked because they contain a greater depth of soil, and retain more moisture, than the surrounding ground. The crop over the old channels will ripen more slowly.

22. London's changing river bank

An interesting feature of this photograph is the group of parallel streets on the right of the river, representing the lines of former river banks. The area between the road on the far right of the picture and the present river bank is all reclaimed land. Excavations carried out in the area by the Museum of London have uncovered a succession of reclamation schemes. Today the edge of the river is well defined and, assuming no catastrophe, unlikely to alter for some time. The photograph also shows a number of London landmarks leading to the large wooded area of Hyde Park at the top of the picture.

23. King's Weir and Lock, Oxon.

A good view of the river meandering across the flood-plain. Flood-plains are not always gently sloping, and weirs and locks may be used to regulate the flow. Locks therefore facilitate the movement of river traffic. The weir belonged in the Middle Ages to Godstow Abbey and is mentioned in a grant of 1541 to the Manor of Wolvercote. It was later owned by the Duke of Marlborough, who also owned the nearby estate of Blenheim Palace. By the beginning of the nineteenth century, the lock had become dilapidated and mechanically unreliable; in 1813 there was an incident when a miller from Wolvercote threw stones at the lock-keeper for refusing to raise the sluices and lower the water level. In mid-century some repairs were carried out, and later the University paper-mills at Wolvercote offered to share the expense of a total reconstruction—although the offer was not taken up. The section of river at the top of the picture is at the highest latitude it attains in its path across the country. Compare the following picture of Weybridge.

← **24. Weybridge, Surrey**

The River Wey, flowing from the left, joins the Thames below Shepperton Lock. This point constitutes the southernmost latitude of the Thames.

25. Teddington Lock, Surrey

Teddington Lock (and Weir), the lowest lock on the river, is the point where the Thames becomes tidal. East of Teddington the river mixes daily with the North Sea. Teddington Lock is also the largest lock system on the river. Over 1,500 million gallons of water pass over the weir every day. There are actually three locks: the Barge Lock, 650 feet long, the Launch Lock, originally built from timber in 1811, 178 feet long, and the Skiff (or Coffin) Lock, built in 1858, which measures less than 50 feet. Just below the locks, the Port of London Authority takes over jurisdiction of the river from the Thames Water Authority (or its official successor).

26. The Tidal Thames

This view looking down the river, with the Belvedere Power Station in the foreground, was taken on a day of unusually clear visibility. The river can be seen meandering through some 30 miles towards Sheerness. This section of the river is tidal, which necessitates special flood protection measures.

27. Marshland on the estuary, Kent

The estuarine marshes of Kent and Essex are a heritage from the ice-age, in the sense that they arose from the drowning of the Thames Valley by the post-glacial rise in sea-level. Land with a low water-table is not necessarily a difficult environment in which to live: at the time of Domesday, the East Anglia fenland was the most thickly populated part of England. However, while inland marsh country can be controlled and profitably worked, coastal marshes cannot be so easily drained and converted, for the water-table is the sea itself. This view shows the tidal channels amongst the sedge grass, and a flood protection wall.

28. Westgate-on-Sea, Kent

Looking east towards Margate and the North Foreland. The cliff is composed of chalk, but is softer than that of the North Foreland (see next plate) and is subject to coastal erosion. Depletion of the cliff has been checked by building a sea-wall at this point. Westgate-on-Sea was a contemporary of Margate in its development as a seaside resort in the late Victorian era.

29. North Foreland, Kent →

The cliffs of the North Foreland stand at the south-eastern tip of the Thames estuary. The land is composed of chalk formed from the skeletons of microscopic sea creatures compacted together and laid down more than 100 million years ago (in the cretaceous period).

The lighthouse standing back from the clifftop was originally constructed in 1683, increased in height in 1793, but reduced again in the nineteenth century. The building on the headland in the centre of the picture was designed in the form of a castle by Lord Avebury, a Victorian politician whose main claim to fame was that he introduced the concept of bank holidays, in 1871. The building has stood in place since 1860.

35

30. Clanfield, Oxon.

One of the earliest visible settlements on the Thames. The concentric-circled enclosure may be the remains of a neolithic causewayed camp. Such camps consist of an area encircled by banks and ditches after the style of forts, but crossed by trackways to facilitate movement. It is known that similar sites existed close by at Abingdon, Staines, and probably at Bray.

The two parallel lines have been claimed to be part of a Roman road crossing the site, although they could also be a more recent trackway. Excavations carried out in the area in 1972 unearthed Iron Age pottery. The dots in the light-coloured area at the centre of the picture could be pits. Only a comprehensive excavation will provide exact information on the nature of the site.

OR at least 1,500 years before the Norman Conquest, the upper Thames flood-plain in the region of Oxford was open grassland. It is said that when an American visitor asked a history professor to show him Oxford's most ancient monument, he was taken outside the city to Port Meadow, where the Thames Valley settlers had been grazing their stock since prehistory.

Chapter 3

Patterns of Settlement

Prehistory

The terms palaeolithic (notionally, from the very dawn of man), mesolithic, and neolithic are the three periods of the Stone Age. The actual dates are of importance in archaeological studies, but must be regarded as only approximate because of the extensive overlap between the ages. Cultural diffusion was a slow process. We may regard the mesolithic period, which followed the palaeolithic, as extending from about 10000 BC up to 4000 BC and overlapping the neolithic from 4500 BC to 2000 BC. Similarly, the Bronze Age culture which followed may be said to have begun to replace the neolithic about 2400 BC.

Some relics of the Stone Age are well known. The Thames Valley includes the site of Swanscombe Man, a pit near the Kent coast of the estuary where were found the earliest human remains discovered in Britain. The most prominent evidence of prehistoric man, the stone circles, represent the final forms achieved in the late Stone Age and early Bronze Age. Evidence from earlier periods includes marks of postholes indicating wooden

construction (for example at Woodhenge, which was discovered from the air near Stonehenge) and pits full of domestic rubbish. Sometimes there are crop marks arising from these disturbances of the soil. The primordial hunter-gatherer societies have left such traces of their winter camps, which were often sited in the river valley.

Farming, and a more stable pattern of settlement, arrived in southern England from the Continent in about 4500 BC. Domesticated sheep and cattle and fields of cultivated wheat appeared in the river valleys. This led to a major change in the landscape, and in the neolithic period the deciduous forests were gradually replaced by fields, clearings, and pastures to the extent that they equalled the area of remaining woodland. Extensive networks of prehistoric fields have been recorded in aerial photographs. Management of the land resulted in a significant increase in the population it was able to support. Indeed the density of earthwork structures in southern England—camps with causeways, henge monuments, and long barrows containing burial remains—suggests a substantial population able to divert manpower into communal projects.

The Bronze Age, extending from about 2400 BC to 800 BC (in the case of southern Britain), has left its obvious traces, not only artefacts such as tools, jewellery, and weapons, but also extensive ground marks resulting from a settled life-style and increasing population. Trade began with the Continent, and the Thames Valley was at the heart of this interchange, with manufacturing centres being set up on the riverside. New inventions and improvements of foreign origin appeared in the valley earlier than in any other part of the country. Proof that a well-developed system of river trading existed in Bronze Age times has come from the excavations beside the Thames at Egham and Bray, where dredging has yielded impressive quantities of metal artefacts, indicating a riverside settlement. Rescue archaeology during the building of the M25 produced clear evidence of substantial settlements by the new Runnymede Bridge. Between Brentford and Battersea, bronze tools, weapons, and ornaments have been found in abundance.

In the succeeding Iron Age the long-distance trading networks continued to develop and the population to prosper. There is evidence of a period after about 400 BC when contact with continental Europe declined dramatically and, except in the south-west peninsula, where they traded in tin, British communities developed in isolation. The traditional view that Britain was profoundly influenced in the Iron Age by migrations from the Continent is no longer universally accepted, since there is no convincing archaeological evidence. However, late in the period, about 75 BC, continental 'Celtic' people, borrowing agricultural technology from Germanic tribes, settled here and for the first time opened to the plough the richest soil in Britain. By 50 BC England was exporting corn to France. Crop marks from this time clearly show up in aerial photographs.

The Iron Age was not a time of peace, however. The defensive structures, still clearly visible in the South-East, in the chalklands of Wessex and the Chilterns, and in the upper and lower Thames areas, support Roman reports of a much-divided country. For Rome, Britain was a rich prize. Demographic maps for that period show an urbanized area around the Thames estuary, extending from Harwich in the north to Folkestone in the south, and all the way up the river to Oxford. This urbanization, the result of intensive cultivation of this naturally rich area in the late Iron Age, proved a magnet for Roman invasion. In AD 43 the forces of Imperial Rome rested in their first winter camp at Rochester.

Roman Occupation

Four centuries of Roman government in Britain, from AD 43 to 410, meant the population was swollen by both an army of occupation and those in the administrative machinery, and the province was forced to contribute to the upkeep of the central bureaucracy in Rome. The richness of the Thames Valley was a reason for continued occupation. The presence of a villa implies a successful farming unit, and clearly there was sufficient profit to support the investment in luxuries such as baths and underfloor heating. The ground plans of these residences can be clearly seen as crop marks. The Romans created landscapes of fields in rigid geometrical patterns in several continental areas, yet in Britain the native field patterns tended to endure.

The Romans are renowned for their achievements in road-building, but they were also skilled in water transport systems. By the time they landed in Britain they had considerable mastery of the techniques for constructing bridges, aqueducts, canals, waterfronts, and water-mills. In particular, they developed London (Londinium) at a site on the northern terraces and flood-plain of the Thames (see chapter 5). Riverside manufacturing and trading therefore developed under Roman rule, and by the fourth century AD large areas of the country were urbanized.

With the collapse of the Roman world, early in the fifth century, came new settlers, collectively known as Angles and Saxons. Aerial photography, which has allowed new interpretation of the patterns of fields and villages, suggests a virtual extermination of the earlier inhabitants by the Anglo-Saxon invaders. In the following centuries the Thames formed the boundary between the territories of two great powers, Wessex in the south and Mercia in the north, which between them occupied most of the country from the south coast up to the Humber.

It had been the agrarian richness of England, compared with other countries, which attracted the Roman Occupation and the successive invasions by Anglo-Saxons and Vikings, and this natural resource continued to govern the life of the country until comparatively recent times.

The open fields of early days, with agriculture a locally organized affair, gradually gave way to enclosed boundaries and increasingly controlled farming practices. Bronze Age enclosures are still detectable here and there, and Iron Age farmsteads are clearly visible in aerial photographs. The habit of enclosing agricultural land continued to effect changes in the landscape, becoming more evident from the thirteenth century onwards and a widespread practice by the turn of the seventeenth century. By 1845 legislation had been passed for nearly 2,800 individual enclosure Acts, and in that year the General Enclosure Act ordered the sweeping changes which produced the squared-off field patterns that we can see today.

31. Gatehampton, Oxon.

This crop mark is showing up as a lusher green than the remainder of the field. The exact purpose of the site is not known, but surface finds indicate that the circles could be part of an Iron Age settlement with its boundary ditch appearing in the bottom right of the picture. The boundary line shows a distinct break which is interpreted as an entrance to the site. Another possible explanation is that the circles constitute a Bronze Age religious site. Both explanations are plausible, but again only a systematic archaeological excavation will provide the answer.

32. Standlake, Oxon.

The village of Standlake probably had its beginnings in the Iron Age, possibly even earlier. The picture shows an area close to the village, with enclosures linked by a trackway. There are a number of crop marks in and around the village, of varying periods, which testify to the almost unbroken period of occupation since the village was first founded.

33. Long Wittenham, Oxon.

This Iron Age settlement was established on what was an island in the middle of the Thames. The river now flows just off the left of the picture, but in prehistoric times part of the river was also flowing down the right of the picture, where its former channel can be seen as a darker pattern in the crop.

Running across the bottom of the picture is a row of dots forming a pit-alignment, that is post holes of vertical supports for a palisade. An entrance may be indicated by the two larger pits in the bottom left of the picture. Since this pit-alignment is built across the downstream end of the island, it probably represents a first line of defence against invaders coming upstream. In the centre of the picture is the settlement comprising a rectangular enclosure and a group of hut circles and pits. The dark green circular marks to the right are probably the remains of earlier, Bronze Age barrows.

34. Long Wittenham, Oxon.

A complex settlement site
consisting of a trackway and
various enclosures. The small
circles mark the territories of huts,
most probably a primitive form of
'damp course'—trenches dug to
limit flooding of the hut floor in
wet weather. The crop marks are
believed to span the period from
the Iron Age up to the Roman.
Romano-British pottery and a
burial ground have been found in
the area close to the top of the
picture.

35. Zouch Farm, Culham, Oxon.

The rectangular enclosures close
to the river bank are believed to
date from the Iron Age. In this
excellent farming country it is
probable that the area has been
farmed continuously ever since.

45

36. Clifton Hampden, Oxon.

Situated on a prominent bend in the Thames, this crop mark is thought to be the surface indications of a Romano-British site. The rectangular feature probably defines a timber building with associated enclosures and pits.

37. Dorchester, Oxon. →

This group of crop marks, in Overy Field, consists firstly of a distinctive pair of parallel lines suggesting a Roman road linking the Roman towns of Silchester and Dorchester. To the left of the lines is an oblong feature believed to be the ditch of a neolithic mortuary enclosure, and further left a complex feature contains a central spot, possibly a grave. The intermediate ring consists of pits or post holes. The other, irregular lines may be the result of enclosures or early field boundaries.

38. Dorchester-on-Thames

Today there is little evidence, either on the ground or viewed from the air, of the original Roman town of Dorocina, an important settlement on the road between Silchester and Alchester. Most of the visible features date from either the medieval period or later, when Dorchester became a market town and a major coaching station on the route between Oxford and Reading. According to the Venerable Bede, in AD 635 Birinus the missionary to the West Saxons baptized the Saxon King Cynegils in the nearby River Thames. Dorchester was Birinus's episcopal seat and remained an important centre of Christianity until the see was transferred to Lincoln after the Norman Conquest. An Augustinian order replaced the secular canons of the former cathedral in about 1140.

The present church is all that remains of the Augustinian abbey, which was dissolved in 1536 by Henry VIII. The residual church, still one of the most prominent features of the town, was purchased for £140 from Henry's Commissioners by Richard Beauforest of Dorchester, who bequeathed it to the parish.

39. Abingdon, Oxon.

Stone Age settlements found nearby testify to how long there has been habitation at this crossing point of the Thames. The picture shows a view of the town from the south-east. It is documented that the river was bridged here in 1416, and that the traffic from Gloucestershire then preferred to cross here rather than at Wallingford. The bridge was extended in the fifteenth century, repaired in 1790, and widened in 1829 to meet the needs of the expanding market town. The latest reconstruction was in the 1920s. To the left of the picture we see the Church of St Helens, largely dating from the Perpendicular period, with a thirteenth-century tower topped by a later steeple. More difficult to see, just to the right of the centre of the picture is the twelfth-century church of St Nicholas, and next to that is the Abbey Close and gateway, dating from 1460 and all that remains after the Dissolution of 1538. Abingdon Abbey was once one of the richest in Britain.

40. Bray, Berks.

The area around the village of Bray has been occupied almost continuously since the Stone Age, and excavations in a gravel pit close to the village have revealed a Bronze Age settlement, an Iron Age farm, and a Roman burial site. The village is built on a bend in the river and contains a number of half-timbered and Georgian houses. Parts of the church date from 1293, but most of the structure derives from a restoration in the mid-nineteenth century. It is best known as the seat of the famous 'Vicar of Bray', purported to be one Simon Alwyn, vicar from 1538 to 1565, who is remembered in the song which tells the story of his survival strategy. Alwyn changed his avowed creed several times, accommodating himself to the religious views of whoever was on the throne.

The Jesus Hospital in the background is an almshouse built around a quadrangle. It was founded in 1627 under the will of William Goddard (d. 1609), a prominent City merchant, for 26 people, 20 of whom had to have lived in the village for a minimum of 20 years each, and be over 50 years of age. The remaining six places were reserved for Freemen of the Fishmongers' Company to administer the charity.

41. Hambleden, Bucks.

Situated at the base of a dry valley in the Chilterns running down to the Thames, Hambleden is one of the most beautiful of the South Buckinghamshire villages. This area was important in the Roman period, and several Roman villas have been discovered in fields adjacent to the village. The centre-piece of the village is the church of St Mary, which dates from Norman times. The church tower collapsed in 1703 and was rebuilt in brick and flintwork in 1721.

42. Roman villa, Hambleden

The term villa is used loosely to describe most Roman houses, and the one shown here was in fact a farm. It was excavated in 1912 and has since been reburied. Today it is visible only occasionally as a lighter outline in a ripening crop of wheat. The villa was built over the course of one of the former river channels of the Thames, which shows up as a darker colour in the crop. An interesting mystery surrounds this particular site: the excavations revealed a total of 97 infant burials alongside the villa, for which it is difficult to provide a convincing explanation.

43. Roman villas, Greenlands, Bucks.

In a field adjacent to Greenlands House are the remains of two Roman villas which show up as parch marks in a field of unripe barley. This photograph was taken during a period of dry weather in June 1989 when the villas were showing up as yellow outlines in the green crop. One building is in the bottom of the picture, and the other is just above the centre. A Roman road can be seen running almost vertically down the right of the picture. The round circular marks are the remains of chalkpits or the scars of uprooted trees.

The Hambleden villa in the previous plate is in a field at the top of the picture, but has not shown up. It is extraordinary that while the villas in this picture have not appeared in previous surveys of the area over the last 15 years, the other villa was clearly visible. The reasons for such variations are complex and not completely understood.

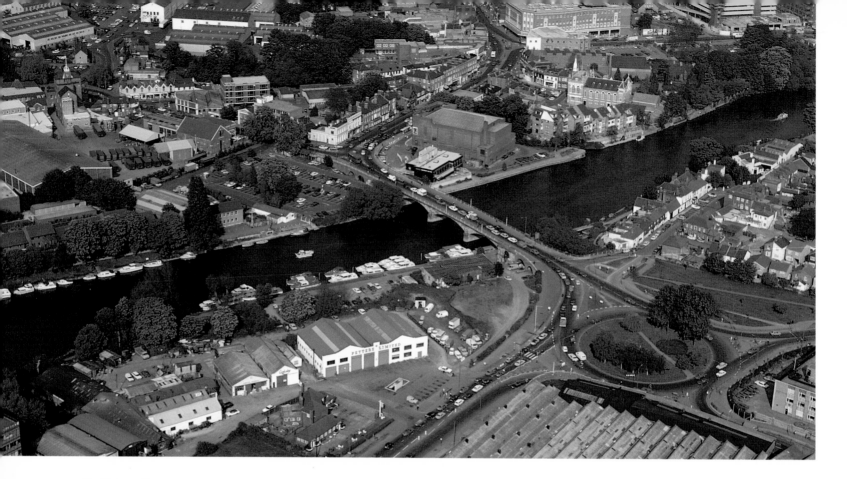

44. Staines, Surrey

Although Staines is now thought of as a London commuter town, and
as such has expanded considerably in the last 30 years, recent
excavations have shown that even in Roman times it was an important
town on the road between Silchester and London. Its connection with
London therefore has a long history.

The Roman road probably crossed the Thames near the present
bridge. Just to the right of the bridge is the old Guildhall, which is where
the wealth of Roman material recently recovered from development sites
in the main street is being processed.

45. Dorney, Bucks.

The two circular features are the ploughed-out remains of Bronze Age round barrows. They were built close to the river and were presumably subject to flooding, as evidenced by the layer of flood silt in this area. It is perhaps surprising that the silt has not obscured the barrow completely. A linear ditch feature overlies the original barrows, and has been found to contain Romano-British pottery. It has been suggested that this ditch was a flood relief or irrigation channel constructed in the Roman period. The dark areas of the crop indicate former river channels. (See also Plate 21 of Dorney.)

46 & 47. Oxford

When the Thames passes through Oxford it carries the special name of Isis. Oxford dates back to the period when Saxons began to settle here in the fifth century AD at a point where the river could be easily forded by their oxen—hence its name. However, aerial photography to the north of the city, over an open space known as Port Meadow, has revealed evidence of settlement going back at least to the Bronze Age and probably earlier.

It is thought that there was a small settlement at the gates of an eighth-century monastery, St Frideswide's, built near the river on the site of the later cathedral in Christ Church. The town, however, like Wallingford, seems to have been deliberately created as part of the Alfredian system of defensive *burghs* or fortified towns. Like Wallingford it was a walled town with a rectilinear plan. Originally it was roughly square with four gates and two principal streets, intersecting at the central crossroads now called Carfax. Before the Conquest the walled area was probably extended on both west and east, and soon after the Conquest Robert d'Oilly built a large castle at the west end, of which the motte survives.

Oxford was an important and flourishing market town long before the University was established. The University began in the twelfth century as an informal association of masters and scholars, perhaps attracted to Oxford by individual teachers in some of the prominent local monasteries. It became organized under a Chancellor in the early thirteenth century, the first college, University College, was founded in 1249, and Oxford soon became a rival to many Continental seats of learning.

The two photographs give an idea of the extent of the city. The first is an overview showing the Isis in the foreground. The second is a view looking westwards across the city centre, showing how much of the central area has been taken over by University and college buildings: it is dominated by the round building known as the Radcliffe Camera, the first library in England to be built on a circular basis. It was constructed in 1748, financed with money left to the University by Dr John Radcliffe, physician to King William III.

← 48. Cookham, Berks.

Cookham is believed to be an early Saxon place-name, and there is archaeological evidence of Saxon settlement in the area. The medieval town developed around the houses on either side of the High Street (in the lower part of the picture). The long house-plots, known as burgage plots, may represent subdivisions of furlongs in an earlier cultivation system. The church in the background has a twelfth-century nave, with additions from the thirteenth and fourteenth centuries. It was probably built on the site of the minster church, which was documented in the eighth century. Many of the High Street buildings date from the fifteenth and sixteenth centuries.

49. Sashes Island, Cookham, Berks.

At the beginning of this century various finds were made on this island which strongly suggest Viking occupation. A number of Saxon weapons have been dredged from the river close to the site, and these may be from attacking skirmishes by native tribesmen.

50. Henley-on-Thames

Henley was a medieval market town, strategically placed at a river crossing. Like at Cookham (Plate 48), the position of the houses along the main street, together with their long gardens, is suggestive of burgage plots cut from open field strips of an earlier settlement. On either side of the main street we see parallel streets which were the back lanes marking the extent of the cultivated strips. Many medieval towns in England can be shown to have developed along such lines.

The bridge over the river was built to the design of William Hayward in 1786. A prominent feature close to the bridge is St Mary's church. It has a tall sixteenth-century tower with interesting flintwork, ascribed to John Longland, who later became Bishop of Lincoln. The churchyard contains the grave of Richard Jennings, Wren's master builder of St Paul's Cathedral.

51. Culham, Oxon.

An interesting example of a 'shrunken village'. In the bottom right of the picture we see the manor-house and church, all that remain standing of the settlement that once existed here. In the field above there are the outlines of a series of streets, hut platforms, and trackways leading down to the river's edge, evidence of the scale of the settlement in medieval times. The decline of such villages was due to a number of factors. The Black Death of 1348–9 is often quoted as the main cause, but it probably only contributed to an already deteriorating village life. In the fourteenth century the English weather became exceptionally wet, harvests failed, and much land under cultivation was abandoned and unworkable. Moreover, landowners were tempted to restructure their farms to profit from the rising price of wool, and large areas of arable land were converted to pasture. Where many men had laboured to raise crops, only a few shepherds were now needed to tend the flocks. In recent years this area has been recultivated, and at the time of photographing the field contained a crop of barley. As previously remarked, barley is an excellent indicator of subsurface features.

61

52. West of Lechlade

The Thames above Lechlade is fairly shallow and not officially open to navigation. The pattern of fields on either side of the river bank is the result of the Parliamentary Enclosure system adopted between 1750 and 1850. Individual statutes transformed the landscape as the Enclosure Commissioners and Surveyors moved from village to village. The irregular, unfenced borders of the old fields were replaced by straight boundaries to provide compact private holdings.

W HAT is developed must be defended, and this is exemplified by the history of Wallingford ('the old fort at the ford'), where a fording point of importance to settlement and trade was a military keypoint for the Saxons, who built defences there, and for the Normans, who built one of the earliest motte and bailey castles to defend the crossing. The 17-span bridge supplanted the ford much later, in an age of wider loyalties—and therefore wider defence issues.

Windsor, which grew up because of its hill and the river, is witness to the same principle. The natural highway of the Thames attracted riverside settlement and water-borne trade, and there was also cross-river traffic. There had been a modest Saxon development at Windsor, but William of Normandy, with an eye to the magnificent hunting forest south of the river, raised a mound (or 'motte') and outer defensive work (the 'bailey') to fortify his acquisition.

The potential of a river as a natural barrier on one or more sides of a stronghold is obvious. Water could form the principal element of defence, it could be a powerful ally of walls and ramparts, or it could be diverted to feed artificial moats. Where a fortress is built close to a river, as indeed many of them were, the fresh water supply would be vital during a siege. The Thames has had many defences constructed along its banks, from its vulnerable estuary right up to its source. Castle Eaton church, on the Wiltshire bank downstream of Cricklade, reminds us in its name of its origins as a guarded crossing of the river.

Before man became civilized, his ceremonial graves,

Chapter 4

Developing and Defending

bearing witness to his life-style in western Europe, contained tools to service the needs of the departed soul. No doubt population pressures prompted the need to defend territory, and the later practice developed of adding the necessary weapons to support the future life. The practice was still in vogue in Saxon times.

There is evidence, clearly visible from the air, of territorial conflicts in southern England as early as 4000 BC. A number of hill-forts occupied a wide arc of land spreading from Sussex through the chalklands of Wessex to the Cotswolds and the Welsh Marches. Significantly, the hill-forts are generally limited to the area stretching immediately south from the Thames: evidently the river itself was an effective barrier. North of the Thames, tribal life was characterized by villages and open settlements. The hill-forts south of the river were to serve their purpose until the end of the Iron Age, when Britain fell to the Roman invasion. The importance of the Thames as a trading route can be seen from the positioning of forts on both sides of the river near Dorchester (Plate 57). If the two forts were in the same hands they would have commanded the river and controlled its traffic.

The Roman legions advanced westwards from their winter camp at Rochester, and looked for a place to cross the Thames. In Caesar's *Gallic War* we read:

I led the army to the river Thames and the territory of Cassivellaunus. There is only one place where the river can be forded, and even there with difficulty. When we reached it, I noticed large enemy forces drawn up on the opposite bank. The bank had also been fortified with sharp stakes fixed along it, and, as I discovered from prisoners and deserters, similar stakes had been driven into the river bed and were concealed beneath the water.

I immediately gave orders for the cavalry to go ahead and the legions to follow them. As the infantry crossed, only their heads were above the water, but they pressed on with such speed and determination that both infantry and cavalry were able to attack together. The enemy, unable to stand up to this combined force, abandoned the river bank and took to flight.

It is believed that the crossing was made at Westminster, the river running at a lesser depth than today, along a broader path.

The Anglo-Saxon invaders who replaced Caesar's organization in Britain had been held off during the Roman Occupation by the 'Forts of the Saxon Shore', established by Rome along the south-east coast in a wide arc centred on the Thames estuary. Initially they settled in coastal areas and the estuary, and later pressed up-river in small boats. In their turn, Viking raiders ravaged large areas of Anglo-Saxon Britain, launching their first attack on Lindisfarne in AD 793, but later turning south towards London. By 850–1, the first year they wintered in England, their fleet in the Thames was estimated by the Anglo-Saxon Chronicle to have reached a strength of 350 ships. In 870 the Viking army moved to a new base near Reading, and began its attack on Wessex. When Alfred came to the Wessex throne in 871, he was forced by the English defeats at Reading and Wilton to sign a treaty which left London and the Thames estuary in Scandinavian hands. Gradually the invaders themselves became settlers, and by 1012 forty-five ships under the Dane Thorkell the Tall had been assigned to the forces of the English King Aethelred, and were stationed on the Thames.

The Norman invasion of 1066 brought an innovation to the design of fortifications with the introduction of the tower, with motte and bailey. William the Conqueror built the Tower of London to dominate the Thames approaches, and the fortress was further developed by the addition of the White Tower, started in 1180, and two rings of walls in the thirteenth century. The Normans constructed fortifications elsewhere on the Thames, for example at Wallingford and Windsor, and at Rochester, where we see a particularly fine example of Norman architecture. The Normans, like the Romans, approached England from the south, and their occupation followed the Roman pattern. Having secured the Thames Valley, their control of the rest of England was assured by the building of castles throughout the country.

In the following centuries the Thames continued to be a military target, and therefore a well-defended one. For example, at Tilbury an anti-invasion blockhouse was built in 1539 in the time of Henry VIII. It was strengthened in the reign of Elizabeth I, and was the scene of her rallying call in the face of the Spanish invasion threats of 1588. In 1667, during the Dutch Maritime War, a Dutch admiral attempted an invasion of England, and his success at carrying the action past the fort at Sheerness underlined the vulnerability of the Thames estuary. The extensive structures erected in the early nineteenth century to counter the threat of invasion by Napoleon are still in place. However, after the time of William the Conqueror no enemy force had penetrated beyond Tilbury until the German air raids of the First World War. In the Second World War, the defences in the Thames approaches included forty sites of heavy anti-aircraft batteries, and the coastal defences were backed up by defence in depth to counter the likely blitzkrieg tactic of fast moving armour covered by air strike. The 'GHQ Line', an echo of the Wessex–Mercia line, still has its visible remains of pill-boxes at Pangbourne, Abingdon, Fifield, and right up to Lechlade, following, unsurprisingly, the Thames.

53 & 54. Wallingford, Oxon.

Seen from above, in the first picture, Wallingford bears a striking resemblance to a Roman town: in fact, it is a planned Saxon fortified town, or burgh. The Saxon settlement occupied the upper part of the picture, with its defences along the curved hedge-line which is most prominent in the centre left.

After the Battle of Hastings, William the Conqueror marched on London, meeting no opposition until he attempted to cross London Bridge. He then followed the south bank of the Thames to the first place where it could be forded—Wallingford. The castle at Wallingford marks that important river crossing: it was one of the first 'motte and bailey' castles to be built under William's authority, by Robert d'Oilly in 1071. The mound, or motte, can be seen on the right of the second picture, and the position of the outer wall, or bailey, is still visible from the air, following the line of trees around the open area in the centre.

A town grew up around the castle but was ravaged by the Plague in 1349, after which only 44 houses remained. The first bridge across the river is believed to have been constructed in 1141, and the present one dates from 1809. In the Civil War, Wallingford was one of the last Royalist strongholds to fall, and after the war Parliament ordered the castle to be destroyed.

In addition to the seventeenth-century Town Hall, Wallingford contains a number of fine Georgian houses. Local residents have successfully campaigned against plans to convert the site of the castle into a building development.

55. Windsor

Windsor Castle can claim the distinction of being the largest in the world. It dates from about 1070 when William I chose the site for the castle on land which was part of the Manor of Clewer. In its original form, it consisted of a motte and two large baileys of timber construction, and it still retains that essential geometry of the Norman style. There was major rebuilding in the reign of Henry II, who died in 1189: by that time the eastern bailey, and the shell keep (a low circular wall) on the site of the Round Tower, were rebuilt in stone. Henry III completed the stone defences, but the external appearance has been changed on several occasions since then. The most extensive alterations were made in the reigns of George IV and William IV by Sir Jeffrey Wyatville.

The original settlement at Windsor was centred around quays and a ford of the Thames. The ford was replaced by a bridge over the river in 1268. The town developed around the castle in the reign of Henry I, with lines of houses appearing to follow the burgage plots of an early cultivation system.

56. Taplow Court, Bucks.

The most interesting feature in this photograph is the large grass-covered mound just to the left of the house. Excavation of the mound during the last century by the Victorian antiquary James Rutland unearthed one of the richest archaeological treasures in Britain: it was surpassed only in 1939 with the discovery of the Sutton Hoo ship burial in East Anglia. The barrow contained the remains of an Anglo-Saxon of considerable importance, probably an area chieftain. The name Taplow is thought to be derived from the Anglo-Saxon, and has been translated as 'the burial of Taeppa', the suggested name of the chieftain. The date given for the burial is *circa* AD 625. The grave contained fragments of gold braid, indicating that the deceased was elaborately dressed for burial, and also gold buckles, glass drinking vessels, a sword, and spearheads, which together with many other objects are now displayed in the British Museum in London.

The house itself, Taplow Court, is of mid-Victorian vintage. It was built for Lord Desborough, one of the major shareholders in the Great Western Railway.

57. Castle Hill, Wittenham Clumps

Situated in a commanding position, overlooking the river to the south of Dorchester in Oxfordshire, this Iron Age hill-fort dates from the second to first centuries BC. The defensive earthworks have been built to take advantage of the steep hill which they encircle. The counterscarp bank has been heaped up from the single deep ditch within the enclosure. The area enclosed by the fort is about nine acres. On the opposite bank of the river, not shown in this photograph, is an equivalent hill which, combined with this one, would have given military control of the river traffic at this point.

58. Reculver Fort

During the later period of their occupation of Britain, the Romans constructed a series of forts to repel Saxon invaders. The first of these so-called 'Forts of the Saxon Shore' was Regulbium (Reculver) on the north-east coast of Kent, erected in the third century AD. The line of forts extended from Reculver to Brancaster in Norfolk, and around the south-east coast to Portchester in Hampshire.

On the south bank of the Thames estuary, Reculver was strategically placed to defend access to the river. Within the fort are the ruins of a church founded in AD 669 by Egbert, the Saxon king of Kent. The twin towers make an important landmark for shipping, and were restored a century ago by the Trinity House organization, which is responsible for coastal navigation aids. There has been considerable erosion of this part of the Thames coastline, and more than half of the fort has been washed into the sea. Coastal erosion continues, and sea defences were further strengthened in 1985.

59. Cricklade

Cricklade, on the upper Thames, is the only Wiltshire town on the river. Once the Roman settlement of Dobunni, it was important during the Saxon period as a frontier town of Wessex. Excavations have dated the defences to the latter part of the reign of King Alfred. According to the Anglo-Saxon Chronicles, in 1016 King Canute came with a force of 160 ships to Cricklade. This is not very plausible unless we accept that they must have been small canoes, since the river is hardly navigable at this point and was probably not any more so a thousand years ago. We should remember that the 'Great Danish Army' which ravaged Britain in the ninth century was measured in hundreds, not thousands.

At the time of Edward the Confessor the town was of sufficient stature to have its own mint. The skyline of the present town is dominated by the Church of St Sampson, which dates mainly from the twelfth century and carries a decorated tower added by the Duke of Northumberland in 1553.

60. Reading

Reading has been an important town since the Saxon period. It is documented in the Anglo-Saxon Chronicle of 870–1, when the Danes are said to have wintered here (presumably having sailed up the river) and repulsed attacks by King Aethelred and his brother Alfred. Its description in the Domesday Book suggests that it had become a town of some significance.

Henry I founded an Abbey here, which was consecrated in 1164. Because of its royal patronage it became one of the principal religious foundations in England, but was dissolved in 1539. Parts of the Abbey remains can just be seen at the bottom of the picture in the centre. In 1150 a castle was built by King Stephen, but this was destroyed in 1152. The mound in the Forbury Gardens (bottom centre) may be the remains of the castle, although it has also been interpreted as part of the Civil War defences. The town's economy was severely disrupted by the Civil War between October 1642 and July 1644, when it was alternately occupied by Parliamentary and Royalist forces.

The importance of Reading as a centre of communication can be seen from the confluence of river, road, and rail systems.

61. Tower of London

One of the most historic fortresses in Europe, initiated by William the Conqueror to protect London from the eastern sea approaches soon after the Norman invasion of 1066. William built the main keep, or White Tower as it is generally known: taking its name, not so much from the white Caen stone used in its original construction, but from the time of Henry III when it was whitewashed both inside and out. Its original form is little changed, but there were some medieval additions, and windows were added by Sir Christopher Wren. Successive monarchs have augmented the fortifications and the Tower has served as both palace and prison. Many illustrious prisoners have been guests here, usually escaping only by way of the executioner's block.

62. Hadleigh Castle

The castle stands on the Essex coastal strip, on a low hill overlooking the Thames. It was completed in 1231 under the initiative of Hubert de Burgh (who had earlier defended Dover against the French in the war of 1216–17), but he fell from favour the following year and his estates were confiscated by the Crown. Hadleigh Castle was improved in the reign of Edward III during the Hundred Years War between England and France. Although situated in a useful strategic position, the castle never saw military action. Anne of Cleves lived here for a while after her divorce from Henry VIII, but later it was reduced to a picturesque ruin by ground subsidence. It was a favourite subject of landscape painter John Constable.

63 & 64. Sheerness Docks and Fort

In the Thames estuary the Isle of Sheppey, separated from the Kent mainland by the shallows of Long Reach, stands over the entrance to the Medway leading to the former naval dockyard at Chatham. The town of Sheerness, on the northern tip of Sheppey, which forms a spur guarding the Medway, is host to the Sheerness Docks and the strategically placed Sheerness Fort.

The first picture is a view of Sheerness Docks looking westwards across the entrance of the Medway to the Isle of Grain power-station. The dockyard was planned by Samuel Pepys, diarist and Secretary to the Admiralty in the reign of Charles II. In 1797 it was the location of the Nore Mutiny, brought about by bad working conditions. It remained a naval dockyard until 1959, and is now a privately owned port. To the left of the docks the group of grey buildings is a steelworks for the manufacture of building reinforcements.

The second picture is a view centred on Sheerness Fort. A blockhouse was built here in 1545 to reinforce the defences of the Thames approaches and in particular to protect the entrance to the Medway. In 1667, during the Dutch Maritime Wars, the position was bombarded, captured, and held while Dutch forces under Admiral de Ruyter probed down the Medway, burned some English shipping, and triumphantly carried off the flagship *Royal George*. This national humiliation triggered the building of additional fortifications with more gun batteries, and in the mid-nineteenth century it was again strengthened, when it was feared that the French under Napoleon III would mount an invasion.

65, 66, & 67. Coalhouse, Cliffe, and Shornemead Forts

The blockhouses (*c.*1540) at Tilbury, Gravesend, and Milton were supported further downstream by those at East Tilbury on the north coast and Higham on the south, both at the bend of the river where it starts to become recognizably an estuary. The Thames Forts (*c.*1800) replaced these blockhouses, but French acquisitiveness and naval rearmament led to the recommendations of a Royal Commission that new forts should be built. The Royal Commission Forts were constructed in the 1870s at Tilbury in the north and New Haven in the south, supported in depth downstream by Coalhouse (near the East Tilbury site), and Shornemead and Cliffe on the south bank opposite Coalhouse. Long before General Gordon was sent to rescue the Egyptian garrison in the Sudan (1884), he was a Royal Engineer officer. He supervised the building of Shornemead and Coalhouse, and is commemorated by the Gordon Promenade, which affords a splendid view of the Thames from Gravesend.

This group of forts, a couple of miles or so downstream of Tilbury and Gravesend, were positioned to bring heavy cross-fire on enemy shipping. The gunports in the curved front of Coalhouse now point to a peaceful riverside park. The Romans, some 1,500 years earlier, treated the defence of the Thames in a similar fashion: running from the Cliffe and Shornemead area, stretching for 140 miles to Rye in Sussex, is the long-distance walk known as the Saxon Shore Way, which follows the line of the anti-Saxon forts built by the Romans in a wide arc centred on the estuary.

68. Tilbury Fort

Tilbury Fort lies downstream of the container port and the town of Tilbury. The sensitivity of the area was underlined in 1380, when a combined French and Spanish fleet landed at Tilbury and Gravesend, burning, looting, and taking prisoners. The road west of Tilbury Fort passes the probable site where Queen Elizabeth I reviewed her troops in August 1588 before the expected arrival of the Spanish Armada.

After the Dutch success in the Medway debacle of 1667, and in recognition of the threat of naval attack, the old Tilbury blockhouse was replaced between 1670 and 1684 by Tilbury Fort, to the design of a Dutch engineer, Sir Bernard de Gomme, Chief Engineer to Charles II. The traditional rounded bastion fort was vulnerable in the final stages of attack, since it was impossible to bring fire to bear close in to the walls—an area of 'dead ground'. The new Tilbury Fort incorporated a defence system, originating in late fifteenth-century Italy, which was based on the angular, star-shaped bastion. This allowed cross-fire right up to the walls. On the inland side, the brick walls are protected by a moat, which could be drained in freezing weather to produce a ditch rather than an ice-covered walkway.

Tilbury Fort does not appear to have suffered any frontal naval attack: however, there were interesting moments. At one period, the reputation of the profession of arms was marred by the scandalous practice of demanding money from ships' masters at gunpoint. Sir John Griffith, Governor of Gravesend, on the opposite bank, was discharged for that offence. State papers of 1690 record the frustration of an attack on Tilbury Fort and Gravesend Blockhouse by '900 Irish', presumably soldiers, championing some unnamed cause. Another incident was the battle of 1776 on the parade ground, arising from a county game of cricket between Kent and Essex and the purloining of arms by the warring players. The garrison troops who tried to intervene suffered one serious bayoneting and one death by gunshot.

69. Ammunition dump

A Second World War ammunition dump in Barking Reach shows up well in this evening photograph, in which the sun helps to highlight the undulations of the ground surface. The flood protection wall has recently been constructed as part of the defence against surge tides.

70. Danesfield House, Bucks.

Danesfield was constructed in 1900 in the Tudor style, within the earthen ramparts of a riverside hill-fort dating from the Iron Age. This photograph was taken in 1974 when the house was still being used by the Royal Air Force. During the Second World War it housed the RAF's Photographic Reconnaissance organization, and it was here that a study of aerial photographs first revealed the presence of the German V1 and V2 missile sites. All the Nissen huts and outbuildings have now been demolished and only the house remains. Sold by the Ministry of Defence, it is used as a company headquarters.

As we have seen, it was geography which drew the Roman legions to London, the first fordable point on the river. On its uneven bed of gravel, clay, sand, and chalk, London is sunk into a depression shaped a million years ago and trimmed into its present form during the earliest ice-age. In the basin, valleys, rivers, and tributaries broke out through the clay from the underlying chalk. There are a number of rivers still feeding the Thames in the London area, most of them buried underground, and we shall return to them in our next chapter.

The Roman city, Londinium, was founded at the confluence of one of those rivers—the Walbrook—with the Thames, in an area not densely populated by native farmers since London clays are not the best ground for crops. A region of scattered homesteads was rapidly transformed under Roman rule into not only Britain's capital city but also its major seaport. Like Rome itself, the city was placed at the lowest crossing place of a major river. The Thames had to be crossed before Colchester could be taken, and the legions needed a secure link on their supply route from the Channel ports. The site was chosen because it was the best place for a bridge.

As a member of an expanding empire which had international trading contacts, Londinium prospered. It had good connections with the interior of the province, and could draw on the exceptional agricultural productivity of the English lowlands. The city enjoyed a surge of commercial vitality which was not seen again for a thousand years. Roman London lies some twenty feet

Chapter 5

London: A Special Place

No, Sir, when a man is tired of London, he is tired of life; for there is in London all that life can afford.

DR SAMUEL JOHNSON, from Boswell's *Life of Johnson*

below the streets we now walk on, but it was only a tiny part of what we now call London: the Roman city being even smaller than the famous square mile of the City of London, which is again a product of the geography of the Thames and its maritime trade. The present City, with a minute residential population swollen daily by an army of office workers, occupies the site of the medieval city which grew beyond the Roman walls.

As Roman power waned, the defensive potential of the Thames became increasingly important. The London Wall protected the city against attack from the north, running from the river at Blackfriars in the west to Cripplegate in the north, and rejoining the Thames just east of the site of the Norman Tower of London. For the river front itself, the Thames seems to have been considered sufficient defence. However, late in the Roman period, about AD 370, the response to the growing threat from the seaborne Saxons was the construction of a massive riverside wall between the wharves and the quays. The ruins of this wall, approximately on the line of the modern Thames Street, were discovered as recently as 1975.

By the time the Romans left, the growing splendour of the Christian Church of Rome was already reflected in England. Moreover, and more significantly, a diffusion of ideas based on humility and exemplified by the emerging monasteries created a faith embraced by all classes, and its deep strength survived the end of empire. The focus of this change in religious style was London, and since

London also had an infrastructure of Government institutions, the marriage of Church and State naturally centred there. Londoners maintained the city as a fortress of decisive importance in the many wars of contending kingdoms that were to come.

The fortunes of the Thames itself were characterized by a number of sudden changes. The geological forces causing the fall, relative to sea-level, of south-eastern England, were irregular, and in a notable period late in the Roman Occupation the waters advanced sharply and damaged trade by flooding parts of the lower Thames and Lea Valleys. In medieval and post-medieval times the river rise was again a significant threat, yet Londoners continued to advance the waterfront, and this added to the natural rise.

London Bridge was vital to London's prosperity as a nexus of trade communications. First built by the Romans using cheaply available wood from the British forests (though they had the technology for properly arched, stone structures), it was renewed in the eleventh and twelfth centuries, but always in wood. In 1176, spurred by Peter of Colchester, Londoners used some of their growing wealth to build London Bridge in stone. The work lasted 33 years, but the bridge lasted six centuries. London wealth was also invested in rebuilding the city's churches, and over one hundred were constructed, the greatest being St Paul's. London Bridge remained London's only road over the river until Westminster Bridge was built in the eighteenth century, by which time the Thames was London's most crowded highway, with passengers in boats threading through the heavy commercial traffic. As the Industrial Revolution gathered momentum, this scene was transferred to London's roads.

With the coming of the railway, the river acquired new bridges to carry the trains. Beneath London there was constructed the world's first underground railway system. The first tunnel to be driven under any river was, initially, part of the overground railway system—on the stretch from Wapping to Rotherhithe. Apart from the growing acreage of railway property, the rapidly expanding docks absorbed large areas of the Thames on the seaward side of London. The London Docks, opened at Wapping in 1805, and the West India Docks, opened in 1808, were the nearest to the city. In 1864 they were amalgamated with St Katherine's Dock, even closer to London.

Attracted by the commercial success of London, its population has grown enormously, to a level where the use of the rail and road networks is an essential adjunct to work. As the population has grown, the rural landscape has steadily disappeared. Observing this process a century ago, Edward Walford, author of *Village London*, wrote:

It has been truly remarked that London is almost daily growing. First come the long monotonous lines of streets and houses, extending on every side, and pushing out arms and feelers in the direction of the country. But far beyond these the builder is busy at his work. He has to meet the wants and wishes of men who seek to combine the advantages of London and of country life. There is a large and increasing class who are not content to be Londoners in the old sense of the word. They must have more space and elbow-room than the close neighbourhood of London can afford. They are impatient of life in a street, and they are driven every year farther and farther afield in search of open and unoccupied ground. In these days of rapid railway communication there is hardly any spot safe from them within reasonable distance of town. They will fix themselves anywhere, so only that there is a railway-station not too far off; and there are very few of the outlying suburbs of London which are not thus suitable for them. But where they settle the charms of the country disappear. What was lately a field is enclosed, and becomes a garden or a private park, from which the public are shut out. Forests are cut down to make room for the new occupants, or are left standing only as far as they are ornamental appendages to the property. This is the sort of process which has been going on for many years past on all sides of London. We may like or dislike it, but we can raise no objection to it. We must take it as part of the general growth of London, and, so viewed, it rises almost to the dignity of a natural law. All that we can ask is that some limits may be assigned to it—that some spots of ground here and there may be kept sacred from intrusion, and may be protected from the flood which is overwhelming all around them.

71. The London Thames

Early morning over London. From our position 1,500 feet above the
Thames, we look down on St Paul's (bottom left), eastwards to Tower
Bridge, and beyond towards the estuary.

72. Houses of Parliament

One of London's most familiar landmarks, the Houses of Parliament are built on the site of the Royal Palace of Westminster, the chief residence of the kings of England from the reign of Edward the Confessor up to Henry VIII. The oldest part of the structure is Westminster Hall (almost in the centre of the picture), built by Richard II between 1394 and 1399. The best-known part, however, is the clock-tower Big Ben on the right of the picture.

Big Ben is in fact the name of the large hour bell, and there are two explanations of how it came to be called this. It could have been named after Sir Benjamin Hall, who was First Commissioner of Works at the time the bell was hung, or, according to other sources, after the prize-fighter Benjamin Caunt, whose exploits led to the term 'Big Ben' being used for a heavy object. The clock came into service on 31 May 1859.

Much of the exterior of the building was designed in the Gothic style by Sir Charles Barry, and the foundation stone was laid on 27 April 1840. The Commons Chamber was destroyed in an air raid on 10 May 1941, and was rebuilt after the war. MPs sat in their new chamber for the first time in October 1950.

← 73. The City of London

The City is the commercial heart of London. The tall black building is the headquarters of the National Westminster Bank, rising through 52 storeys to a height of just over 600 feet, making it the tallest building in Britain. To the left, the tall grey building is the new Stock Exchange. In the foreground there is Tower Bridge, and to the right of that is the Tower of London.

The Thames has been bridged at the point called London Bridge many times since the original Roman structure, made of wood, was put up. The bridge in this photograph (the next up from Tower Bridge) was built in 1973 from pre-stressed concrete. The previous bridge, dating from 1901, was carefully dismantled and re-erected at Lake Havasu City in Arizona, USA.

Moored in the river between Tower Bridge and London Bridge lies the cruiser HMS *Belfast*: launched in 1936, she has been restored and converted into a floating museum.

74. Tower Bridge

The furthest downstream, and probably the most famous of all the Thames bridges, Tower Bridge is a very attractive subject for aerial photography. Designed by Sir John Wolfe Barry and Sir Horace Jones in 1886, it was opened in 1894, by which time it had cost the City Corporation over one million pounds. The two towers are 200 feet high and 200 feet apart. The centre span can be raised to allow larger ships to move up to the Port of London, a relatively infrequent event now that the bulk of London's dock activity has moved downstream.

75. Albert Bridge

Crossing the Thames at Chelsea is the graceful suspension bridge designed by Rowland Ordish in 1873. The distance between the supports at the ends of the bridge is 710 feet, with a centre span of 383 feet. The bridge is interesting from an engineering point of view, because it embodies features of both suspension and cantilever principles. In recent years this and adjacent bridges have been skilfully painted in order to highlight their Victorian embellishments.

76. Rotherhithe

Just behind the church in the centre of this photograph is a circular structure which might go unnoticed. It is part of the tunnel shaft and engine house of Isambard Kingdom Brunel's famous Thames Tunnel, which was completed in the face of many daunting problems. The tunnel was originally conceived as a pedestrian way, but in 1865 it was opened to carry the railway under the Thames between Rotherhithe and Wapping. That section of rail is shown on the London Underground map as part of the East London Line. The engine house was restored in 1980.

The church is the Church of St Mary. It was built in the early part of the eighteenth century, much of it by shipwrights, and the columns are made from tree trunks. On the left of the picture we see some of the riverside warehouses at Wapping. Formerly such warehouses stood on both sides of the river right into the heart of London: they have largely disappeared in recent years with the extensive redevelopment of the riverside.

77 & 78. Waterloo

Waterloo is the terminus for trains serving the south coast of England. The original station was opened in 1848, though the present structure dates from 1922. To the left in the first photograph is the area redeveloped for the 1951 Festival of Britain. All that remains of the event is the Royal Festival Hall, which is partly obscured by the tower of the Shell Building—the white high-rise building in the top left. The two bridges in that corner are the Hungerford railway bridge and Waterloo Bridge. The next building round from Waterloo Bridge is the National Theatre, which has been subject to differential weathering of its exposed surfaces and has attracted much criticism.

The three ships moored on the opposite bank of the river are the *Wellington*, *Chrysanthemum*, and *President*. The *Wellington* is the floating headquarters of a City livery company; the other two are used as marine training vessels.

The second picture provides another perspective of the area, with Waterloo Bridge in the foreground and the Royal Festival Hall bottom right. Waterloo Bridge was officially opened in 1945, replacing an earlier bridge constructed in 1817.

79. St Katherine's Dock

The docks closest to the last bridge on the river, Tower Bridge, are
St Katherine's. Not unexpectedly, they were one of the first to become
redundant with the introduction of containerization and the movement
of unloading points down the estuary. With work starting in 1827,
using a labour force of 2,500 men, the docks were completed in 1828.
The area has been redeveloped in the last twenty years and today
St Katherine's Dock contains the Historic Ship Collection. The large
vessel in the bottom right of the photograph is Captain Scott's *Discovery*,
shortly before it was moved to Dundee.

80. Southwark Cathedral

Caught between a railway viaduct
and derelict warehouses,
Southwark Cathedral did not
present an appealing view at the
time this photograph was taken,
several years ago. Since then,
most of the warehouses have been
demolished and the area
redeveloped. The Cathedral was
developed on the site of a
seventh-century nunnery, which
became a church in 1106. It was
the local church of the players in
the Globe Theatre, and
Shakespeare's younger brother is
buried here.

Excavations by the Museum of
London in the area adjacent to
where the white van is parked in
the courtyard (top right) have
revealed evidence of extensive
Roman settlement on the south
bank of the Thames.

81. Battersea Church

The present Battersea Church stands on one of the earliest consecrated sites on the south bank of the Thames, a gift by William the Conqueror to the Abbot of Westminster in 1067. The church was rebuilt in 1777, and its main claim to fame is that the landscape artist Turner painted his sunset pictures of the Thames from the vestry window.

Behind the church there are flour mills and a grain silo, built at the turn of the century when much grain was being shipped up the river from continental Europe and America. Many of the mills on the south bank have been demolished in recent years under redevelopment programmes.

82. Lambeth Palace

The official residence of the Archbishop of Canterbury, the palace is believed to have been founded by Archbishop Boniface in 1216. Cardinal Morton made many additions prior to 1500, including the gateway near the church in the bottom right-hand corner of the picture. Amongst the palace's notable residents have been Cardinal Wolsey and Archbishop Thomas Cranmer. Ironically, next to the palace, in the bottom right of the picture, is a redundant church: Lambeth Church, which was rebuilt in 1851 with the exception of its tower, a survival from the original construction. It contains the tomb of Captain Bligh, notorious for his role in the Mutiny on the *Bounty*.

83 & 84. Greenwich

Royal Greenwich belonged in the fifteenth century to Humphrey, Duke of Gloucester. Henry VIII was born here, and so were his daughters, Mary and Elizabeth.

The group of buildings in the centre of the first picture are well known for their symmetry and harmony of styles—actually the work of several architects, including Inigo Jones, Sir Christopher Wren, Sir John Vanbrugh, and Nicholas Hawksmoor. Furthest from the river is the Queen's House, a small palace which now forms part of the National Maritime Museum. The four quadrangled buildings leading to the river's edge comprise the Royal Naval College. The original conception was a palace for Charles II, but the Great Fire of London put a stop to further expansion and the building was developed into a hospital for naval

pensioners. In 1873 it became the Royal Naval College, and its palatial Painted Hall used as a dining-room as originally intended. It was in this hall that the body of Admiral Lord Nelson lay in State. Situated on the eastern side of London ('buzz-bomb alley'), Greenwich was well placed to experience and observe the great fires of the Second World War. The second picture shows the Royal Naval College in the top left, and in the centre we see the famous tea-clipper, the *Cutty Sark*, in its dry dock alongside the small yacht *Gypsy Moth IV*, in which Sir Francis Chichester became the first person to sail single-handed around the globe. On the right, further up-river, a vessel is moored in preparation for one of the Tall Ships races.

85. Trafalgar Square

Admiral Lord Nelson's flagship, HMS *Victory*, was constructed on the Medway at Chatham Dockyard. The hero of the Battle of Trafalgar in 1805, he was buried in St Paul's Cathedral in a coffin originally made for King Henry· VIII.

Trafalgar Square was designed by Nash, and Nelson's Column erected in 1841. The Corinthian column is $167\frac{1}{2}$ feet tall, surmounted by a $17\frac{1}{2}$ ft statue of the Admiral. At the base of the column are four large lion statues designed by Sir Edwin Landseer; they were installed in 1868 in the midst of considerable criticism over their expense. The fountains were an afterthought, added in 1845 to the design of Sir Charles Barry and carved from Peterhead granite.

In the bottom right of the picture is the National Gallery, which was started in 1824 with 38 paintings purchased from a private owner. At the top of the picture is the distinctive curved profile of the Admiralty Arch, designed as a memorial to Queen Victoria.

BEGINNING as a corridor of invasion and
settlement, developing slowly into a trading
outlet to the seaway, the Thames Valley is now a
major commercial area with a network of roads, railways,
airports, and container ports. In this chapter we shall
review the development of the Thames as a transport
facility for trade, as a source of water services (for
domestic, agricultural, and industrial purposes), and the
effect of these enterprises on our environment.

In a country with navigable rivers, travel favoured the
river valley, and the river itself as the most practical
means of bulk movement. Until the building of hard,
all-season roads, the advantages of river travel remained.
The construction of hard roads and railways is of course
easier on level or only gently sloping ground, and they
are inevitably built along the paths favoured by the rivers.
The first public railway was built between London and
Bristol, serving areas of the Thames Valley which had
relied on the river as a highway since prehistory. The
Goring Gap, where the Thames makes its way between
the chalk hills of the Chilterns and the Berkshire Downs,
has been a key transport feature from time immemorial.
The ford here provided a vital link between two important
ground tracks, the Icknield Way and the Ridgeway.
Today, the road and railway also go through the Goring
Gap, affording modern travellers the benefit of that scenic
route.

In negotiating the Goring Gap the railway crosses two
bridges over the Thames. As an architectural form, the
bridge has experienced less evolutionary change than

Chapter 6

The Changing River

It is upon the sea coast, and along the banks of navigable
rivers, that industry of every kind naturally begins to
subdivide and improve itself

ADAM SMITH, *An Enquiry into the Nature and Causes of the
Wealth of Nations* (1776)

almost any other type of construction. Medieval pack-horse bridges were not strikingly different from those built at the start of the nineteenth century. It was only the introduction of new materials—cast-iron, steel, and concrete—and the development of new engineering techniques exploiting them, which transformed the traditional outlines of the bridge into a heavy-load-bearing, high-arched structure providing transport across a river without obstructing traffic up and down.

Rivers and other bodies of inland water are an extension of the maritime environment, and even now, when an increasing amount of cargo is moved by aircraft, our seaports are the gateways through which 95 per cent of our exports and imports (by volume) are delivered. It is still cheaper for freight to travel by sea than by air. The ports of the Thames estuary constitute one of Europe's leading centres of maritime trade. The major port facilities have gradually moved downriver, seeking both deeper water and less expensive land. Some of the most impressive developments have been at Tilbury, where the world's largest container terminal for refrigerated ships was completed in 1978. Here ships are accommodated in one of the largest docks in England, 1,000 feet long and 110 feet wide. Even so, soon after its construction it could only just take the largest container ships in use. Further down the river is Canvey Island oil refinery, just east of Cooling Marshes, opened by BP to accept crude oil from the Middle East and more recently the North Sea. The move downriver left derelict that monument to the Industrial Revolution, the London Docks. The opportunity

has not been wasted, however, and the effects of a positive environmental policy backed by commercial drive are very visible from the air. The dockland area is becoming commercial again and, by March 1988, 5.2 million square feet of office space had been completed, with another 5.9 million square feet under construction. New dwelling units had already attracted an influx of some 60,000 new residents into an area of eight square miles, and an increase in the working population of about ten times that figure is expected.

The Thames receives the drainage of more than one-seventh of the area of England, and has become one of the most intensively used rivers in the world. Water is removed for drinking in towns such as Swindon, Reading, and Slough, and after sewage treatment is returned to the river to be drunk again further down. London is at the end of the line. Management of the resource is a delicate business. At the time of writing, Thames Water is the world's largest water authority, responsible for managing the total water system in an area of 5,000 square miles, comprising some 1,600 miles of rivers and water courses, and serving the needs of 11.5 million people. The region also caters for 27 million tourists every year. The territory of Thames Water coincides with the geographical area of the Thames Basin. The other water systems draining into the estuary derive from the coastal regions of Kent and Essex, but these are not the responsibility of Thames Water.

Thames Water supplies water for household and industrial use, for growing crops, and for recreation.

Every day, 1,000 million gallons are required to meet the demands, backed by a reservoir capacity of over 50,000 million gallons. In the region are more than 90 water-treatment works: these test, treat, and regulate the quality of the water, which is then pumped through a network of 26,000 miles of water-mains.

From the Roman Conquest until the introduction of steam power, moving water provided the main source of industrial energy in Britain. The average fall of the Thames (dubbed by our Celtic ancestors 'Tamos'—the gentle river) between the source and Teddington, where it becomes tidal, is about two feet per mile. This hardly provides a torrent for energy conversion. However, local changes in the landscape, both natural and induced by riverside management schemes, have required locks to be built for navigation, and water-mills were installed to take advantage of local falls. Few medieval water-mills have survived intact, but many later mills occupy early sites, and the mills at places like Hambleden on the Thames date from the time of Domesday. Overall, most of the 5,500 English mills recorded in the Domesday Book survive—but only as ruins.

Power generation is still strongly associated with rivers. Thermal stations draw in water for cooling purposes and release it at a higher temperature. This can be harmful to the river and its freshwater life in several ways. In particular, the oxygen-carrying capacity of the warmer water is reduced, and this accelerates the anaerobic decay of organic matter. Heated water discharged in an area already polluted can have disastrous ecological effects.

Until the Industrial Revolution, Nature was not overwhelmed by our demands on our rivers. The situation has dramatically deteriorated. With the changes in agriculture, the rapid expansion of population and industry over the last hundred years, and increasing recreational demands, many of our freshwater lakes and rivers have become denatured. However, over a twenty-year programme, control and prevention of pollution is now paying off. In particular, over 100 species of fish have returned to the tideway, and salmon are again leaping in the Thames. While, no doubt, the river could be still cleaner, at least the tidal Thames can now boast that it is the cleanest metropolitan estuary in the world.

Attempts at river management have been recorded from Roman times. Originally when the Thames flooded, the deposit of silt across the valley gradually raised the valley floor and so limited the severity of future floods. This was a natural form of control, though not conducive to a quiet life for those in a riverside settlement. Roman efforts to control the river deprived the flood-plain of these silt accumulations, while the drying and draining of riverside land lowered its surface by up to three feet, greatly enlarging the area which would be inundated should the river ever burst its man-made limits.

Irrigation and drainage are the life-blood of agriculture. Fertile valleys are natural sites, and although early developments might favour adjoining high ground rather than marshy riversides, successful farming practices are inevitably linked to proper river management.

Increasingly over the past two centuries, our agricultural landscape has been manipulated in order to economize the use of labour rather than land. Forty years ago, about one-third of the working population in Western Europe were engaged in agriculture, a dramatic fall since pre-industrial times, but in England the figure was already below 6 per cent. It has now fallen to a level of about 2½ per cent. The average cereal field contains one working man on twelve days of the year. Our view, as we fly over the farmlands of the Thames Valley, is of a countryside rich in crops but empty of people.

Long after the last ice-age, the land mass of Britain continues to tilt down, slowly, at the south-east end. In spite of work over many centuries, including the building of river levees, the risk of flooding from the seaway has steadily increased to a serious level. It was the growth of the conurbation of London that made the problem acute, and the Thames Barrier, which contains the risk at an acceptable level, now gives the city essential protection. The pattern for disaster is a high tide driven by strong winds along the northerly length of the North Sea into the Thames estuary, and in recent times the 1953 tide surge is well remembered on the east coast. It is calculated that this surge would have been contained (from the Londoner's point of view) by closure of the Thames Barrier over a period of two tides. Further down the river, the flood barriers at Barking Creek and Dartford Creek provide protection for residential and industrial sites in those areas.

The flood risk arises because London lies in an alluvial plain formed by the meandering Thames, the northern banks of which rarely rise over thirty feet above the river, and the southern banks of which are reclaimed marshland. There are hundreds of miles of smaller rivers in London, which once flowed through meadows. Villages grew on their banks; as London grew the villages turned into suburbs and the rivers into sewers. Those rivers are now buried, but their names are remembered: on the north side of the Thames, Stamford Brook, Counter's Creek, Westbourne or Ranelagh, King's Scholars Pond or Tyburn, the Fleet, Walbrook (with its early Roman connection), Shoreditch, Hackney Brook, Black Ditch, and the Lea (or Lee). On the south side of the Thames, Beverley Brook, the Wandle, Graveney, Falcon Brook, Effra, and the Ravensbourne with its own cluster of streams including the Pool, Quaggy Brook, and Kid Brook. The Westbourne began at Hampstead, formed a loop we now call the Serpentine, and ran through Chelsea: it still does, in a metal box over the platform at Sloane Square Underground Station. These rivers are now lost beneath us, and lost with them is another London we shall never see again. Although of course the rivers sometimes administer sharp surprises, for example springing from the ground during excavations for the foundations of buildings.

The most striking feature of lowland rivers is the richness of their habitats for a variety of life. The effect on these rivers of man's activities has been to reduce the variety of plant and animal life, which may be a convenience in the cause of productivity but can also be a short-sighted policy. Since man is part of Nature, it is hardly logical to define the environment in terms which exclude human activity, and our river management systems, some of long-lasting effect, are part of our natural heritage. Changes, some good, some bad, continue under the commercial and social drives of this century. Individual changes may be small, but cumulatively the impact on our environment assumes an exponential form. Even those who are professionally concerned sometimes have difficulty in grasping the scale of the changes. While much good work has been done in the London Docklands, and in the biological cleaning of the river, nevertheless the naturalist and the environmentalist will claim that most of the changes have been bad. We can certainly see examples of serious degradation in the Thames area. W. G. Hoskins, in his classic work *The Making of the English Landscape*, sees the extending finger of later industrialism in this way:

Nor are the worst of modern industrial landscapes in the traditional areas. One of the most depressing parts of England is the north side of the Thames Estuary around Thurrock, best viewed from the M25, travelling fast. Even 19th century industrialists at their worst did not quite approach this.

There is still room, and there is still time, to come to terms with a limited natural resource, and through foresight and restraint ensure that our heritage is respected and enjoyed.

86. Isleworth, Middx.

In the seventeenth and eighteenth centuries, Isleworth was a residence
for London commuters. They travelled by river rather than use the
roads, which could be choked with mud in winter. Villages like
Kensington were often cut off. The main street of Isleworth, shown here,
dates from those times, and the church was built even earlier, with a
tower added in the fifteenth century.

87. Goring

The town of Goring lies on a section of the Thames which separates Berkshire from Oxfordshire. Although prehistoric and Roman artefacts have been found here, indicating long-term settlement, the village was probably redeveloped in the Saxon period. Goring is mentioned in the Domesday Book as 'Goringes', the same name appearing later in a deed of 1277. At the time of the Norman Conquest, Goring was held by Wigod, the Saxon Thane of Wallingford.

Goring church, centre right in this photograph, is largely of the twelfth century. The river lock has long been a feature of the town, and can be seen on the left. In 1538 a Mr Stoner was granted a ferry and weir, i.e. a flash-lock, which is essentially a device for damming the river flow: on lifting the gate, the flash of water carries the barge across the shallows in exciting style. A pound-lock was built in 1787, with the now common two-gate device (enclosing the pound containing the barge). This allows a more gentle transfer between levels. In 1837 a bridge was constructed across the river, which was rebuilt in concrete in 1922–3.

88. Pangbourne

This point on the course of the Thames through Berkshire is of special interest. Here, the river, road, and railway all converge to pass through the Goring Gap in the south of the Chiltern Hills. Near this spot lived Kenneth Grahame, author of *Wind in the Willows*.

89. Maidenhead, Berks.

The bridge in the foreground was built by Isambard Kingdom Brunel to carry the Great Western Railway over the Thames. It was an innovative design, with two of the largest and flattest arches ever constructed in brickwork, each with a span of 128 feet. The project was not without problems: in May 1838 when the timber supports were eased, an arch subsided because the cement had not properly hardened between the bricks. Part of the arch was rebuilt, but Brunel's critics were convinced it would collapse. The following spring, the supports were washed away in a violent storm. To the triumph of Brunel the bridge did not collapse, and it has carried the railway over the river ever since.

In the background is Maidenhead Road Bridge, on the London–Bath road, constructed in 1772-7. Tolls were collected from users until 1903, when the toll-gates were dismantled and thrown into the river by angry local residents.

There has probably been a crossing at this point since the Stone Age. Archaeologists diving in the river have found numerous flint axes of the neolithic period, suggesting that it was a crossing worth defending.

90. Gatehampton Railway Bridge, Berks.

The Great Western Railway between Bristol and London followed the flat ground west of the Chilterns and crossed the Thames at Gatehampton. It then ran parallel with the river to converge with it at Goring. During its construction, Roman remains were found on the south bank of the Thames at Lower Basildon (see Plate 9, which shows crop marks and the ground preparations for the bridge). The Gatehampton Bridge, which has been relatively maintenance free, still carries modern rail traffic.

91. Newbridge

Newbridge, well up-river in Oxfordshire, is in fact one of the oldest bridges on the Thames. It dates from about 1250, but was largely rebuilt in the fifteenth century and repaired in 1901. The stone used in its construction came from Taynton Quarry, some 14 miles to the north-west, and is the same stone as was used for St George's Chapel, Windsor. Newbridge was captured by Cromwell during the Civil War, in 1644.

At either end of the bridge there is a public house: on the left of the picture, the Maybush Inn, and on the other side of the river, the Rose Revived. The bridge at one time served an important social purpose because, as a result of local government bureaucracy, the two inns had different licensing hours.

92. Marlow

←

The suspension bridge which crosses the river at Marlow, in Buckinghamshire, was built in 1831–6. It was designed by William Clarke as a prototype of the bridge which was later built over the Danube at Budapest. Marlow Church was rebuilt in 1832–5, and the spire added in 1898. Within the church is the tomb of Sir Miles Hobart, a Roundhead who is immortalized by what is claimed to be the first monument to be erected in England by public subscription.

93. Greenwich Observatory

In 1423 Humphrey, Duke of Gloucester, enclosed Greenwich Park and built a watch-tower on the north-facing hill above the river. This was to become the site of the Greenwich Observatory.

The history of the observatory is part of the history of marine navigation. The invention of the marine chronometer by John Harrison and the introduction of the *Nautical Almanac* in 1766 by the Astronomer Royal Nevil Maskelyne led many mariners to use Greenwich time and the Greenwich meridian. For resetting seagoing clocks, the signal was usually a Time Ball, visible through a ship's telescope, dropped at a fixed time each day in the main ports—this began in Greenwich, for the ships on the Thames, in 1833. Radio technology has of course changed the means of communication, but Greenwich Mean Time, based on the Greenwich meridian, which by definition runs through the Greenwich Observatory, was accepted as the international standard in 1884.

The Royal Observatory, dating from 1675, was designed by Christopher Wren, who recommended its location for astronomical observation. Its largest telescope is a 26-inch refractor, but the effectiveness was always limited by the humidity of the Thames shoreline, and increasing air pollution led to the transfer of most observational work to Herstmonceux, in East Sussex.

Apart from the importance of the observatory in support of accurate navigation, the area has other military connections. At nearby Woolwich there was a naval dockyard, which was established in Tudor times and remained Britain's chief dockyard until the advent of the 'Ironclad' warship. It closed in 1869. Close to the observatory is the church of St Alfege. Archbishop of Canterbury in the eleventh century, Alfege was taken prisoner by the Danes, who beat him to death on the spot where the church now stands.

94. Tilbury container port

In the early 1970s there was a revolution in the handling of sea-borne goods. The introduction of sealed containers had a dramatic effect on London's dockland: the traditional docks were run down as large container ports were established on the east coast at Felixstowe and on the estuary here at Tilbury. Some 25 miles downstream from London Bridge, and ideally situated to handle the European container trade, Tilbury is now the third largest container port in Britain.

95. Canvey Island refinery   →

The flat expanse of Canvey Island and its petrochemical works. Situated close to Southend, the island is in the tidal reaches of the Thames. The construction of sea-walls and drainage channels has lessened the flood risk, but the surge tide of 1953 drowned 58 people. Massive new concrete defences, with steel floodgates, now guard both population and industry.

96. Gravesend

The industrialization of the Thames estuary is evident from this picture, taken from above the Gravesend area on the Kent coast, with the town on the left. The chimneys of cement works, power-stations, and factories can be seen on both banks of the river.

The line of tugs moored in the river (left of centre) represent a declining trade. The tugs are used to escort larger vessels up-river, but the present trend is to redeploy docks downstream, away from the heart of London, to areas of deeper water and cheaper land, and closer to the shipping approaches. The Port of London's Thames Navigation Service has its headquarters at Gravesend: from below its radar-turreted building the pilot boats work from the Royal Terrace Pier, guiding shipping from Gravesend upstream to Tilbury and beyond.

97. Brentford Dock

The ford of the river Brent is no longer in evidence. Nearby there is a granite column recording an event of military significance. Here, it is claimed, British tribesmen unsuccessfully opposed the Roman crossing of the Thames in 54 BC.

Built on part of the site of the old Brentford Dock, the development in this photograph includes a small marina with moorings. This is the point where the Grand Union Canal joins the River Thames. Once a thriving commercial waterway, the canal is now used mainly by pleasure-craft. Indeed, many of the old narrow boats provide the opportunity for tranquil holidays.

98 & 99. Newham Docks and the City Airport

This group of three docks, east of London, once comprised the largest on the Thames. Top left in the first picture is the Royal Victoria, completed in 1855. It was followed by the Royal Albert (centre right) in 1880 and the King George V (centre left) in 1921. Great passenger liners, including the *Mauretania*, were refitted here before the Second World War.

The first photograph shows the docks as they were towards the end of their use in 1985. In 1987 the buildings along the centre strip were demolished to make way for the City Airport, shown in the second picture.

Squeezed into the area of the disused Newham Docks, the airport was constructed to a length of 762 metres plus an over-run at each end. It was opened by HM the Queen on 27 October 1987. Closely surrounded by buildings, the airport is used by aircraft with high angles of approach and climb. They must also have a relatively low speed and light capacity, in order to brake safely on the short runway. The cost per passenger is therefore relatively high and, since a fast transport link with the City of London is not yet in place, usage remains low.

100 & 101. Isle of Dogs

The first picture shows the dock area in 1983, before it was redeveloped. We can see clearly how the river meanders around the Isle of Dogs.

In the centre right of the picture there are the disused West India Docks, built on the authorization of Parliament in 1799 because the Port of London had become overcrowded. Construction by William Jessop under the auspices of the West India Company was rapid, and two docks were completed by 1802. In 1870 the south dock (the left of the group of three) was completed: it was built over the site of the City Canal, which linked Limehouse Reach and Blackwall Reach (above and below), between 1805 and 1824. The docks just left of centre, at the south end of the Isle of Dogs, are the Millwall Docks, which were completed in 1864. Tower Bridge can be seen in the distance.

The Isle of Dogs is being redeveloped at an extraordinary pace. Once an area of dilapidated housing and redundant docks, in a scheme costing many millions of pounds it is being totally transformed. The second picture, taken in 1989, gives some idea of the changes that are taking place around the West India Docks.

102 & 103. Millwall and West India Docks

The first picture is a view of the Millwall Docks from 1975, showing ships in the docks and moored alongside. The second picture, taken in 1986, shows the new development around the Millwall and West India Docks, which was completed in 1984. In the foreground on the right is the new *Daily Telegraph* building.

104. Boulter's Lock, Berks.

For many centuries the Thames was a working river, providing water-power to operate mills. Boulter is an old word with two meanings—a type of fishing line, and a person who sieves grain. In this case the latter meaning is most likely: the mill on this site was known as Ray's Mill, after Richard Ray, who was the lock-keeper before his retirement in 1829. The lock, which is near Maidenhead, was originally constructed in 1770, and has a fall of almost eight feet, second only to Teddington Lock at the tidal gateway of the Thames.

105. St John's Lock →

The furthest lock up the river, which still has its paddles raised by a windlass, is St John's at Lechlade in Gloucestershire. First constructed in 1789, it has been rebuilt on several occasions since. St John's Bridge, adjacent to the lock, originates from 1229. In front of the lock is Rafaelle Monti's statue of *Old Father Thames* (see Plate 145).

106 & 107. Temple Mill Island, Berks.

The island, by Temple Lock, takes its name from the Knights Templar, who held the nearby Bisham estate (see Plates 133 and 134). Later, the monks of Bisham Abbey held the riverside Temple Mills as part of their estate. First used for corn milling, around 1710 the mills became a foundry for converting copper into brass. In 1788 they were enlarged and modernized by the architect Samuel Wyatt, and copper was then brought to the site from Swansea via the newly opened Thames and Severn Canal. In 1848 the mills started the manufacture of brown paper, finally closing in 1969.

The first photograph was taken in 1974. The mill area was subsequently demolished, and the island redeveloped as a small marina surrounded by luxury houses, as shown in the second photograph.

108. Farmoor Reservoir, Oxon.

In the countryside near Eynsham, by Pinkhill Lock, lies Farmoor Reservoir, completed in 1977 with a capacity of some 370 million gallons. It supplies water to Oxford and as far afield as Bicester, Chipping Norton, and Swindon, drawing up to 30 million gallons per day from the Thames. In the right of the photograph there are hedges of medieval fields which have so far escaped conversion to the large, open field plans of modern agricultural practice.

109. Platt's Eyot, Surrey

An eyot is an island. Behind this island in the Thames, on the left of the picture, is the Hampton Pumping Station, where water is pumped from the river and passed through filter-beds. It is said that by the time the water reaches this point in the river it has already been drunk five times by consumers upstream.

110. Thames Barrier

One of the latest sights on the river, the Thames Barrier has become a popular tourist attraction on boat trips from Westminster Bridge. The largest movable barrier in the world, it was completed in 1982 at a cost of 450 million pounds. It is said that the bedrock of south-eastern England is sinking at a rate of about 30 cm per hundred years, and the effect is exacerbated by global warming causing a general rise in sea levels. If an intense depression forms over the North Sea, high winds may drive surface waters over the long sea track from the Norwegian Sea to the Channel, and form a surge tide in the Thames estuary. In 1953 a flood in the estuary drowned 300 people and provided a dramatic warning of the threat to the population of Greater London. Initially the threat was addressed by raising the level of the river banks, but with another serious flood in 1971 it was realized that further measures were required.

After consideration of several possible schemes, contracts for the Barrier were awarded in 1974. A series of massive concrete piers were built across the river and linked with curved steel barriers, which normally lie flush with the river-bed but can be rotated to raise their flat faces vertically against the river flow. The largest pair of steel sectors weigh 1,400 tonnes each. The Barrier was completed just in time: in February of the following year (1983), it was first raised in response to a threat of widespread flooding.

111. Dartford Creek Barrier

The tidal surge barrier at Dartford Creek is linked with the overall flood protection scheme associated with the Thames Barrier. If circumstances cause the Thames Barrier to be raised from its position on the river-bed, then the Dartford Creek Barrier will be lowered at the same time to prevent a surge from flowing up the creek. The photograph shows Dartford Creek in the foreground, and the barrier at the junction with the Thames.

The town of Erith is on the left of the picture, with Thamesmead in the far distance. Belvedere power-station is on the bend of the river, centre right (see also Plate 118).

112. Barking Creek Barrier

Barking lies some nine miles east of central London. In the early part of
the nineteenth century, it was one of Britain's principal fishing ports.
But then the railways came. In the mid-1860s the railway reached the
east coast ports of the North Sea and provided easy transport from
unloading points close to the fishing grounds. Today there are schemes
to build overflow housing for the London conurbation at Barking Reach,
including some prestigious waterfront houses, and a business park to
nurture new industries.

The Barking Creek Barrier, seen here in its normal, open position,
protects the area by blocking the rising water-level of the estuary.

113. Southend →

Southend-on-Sea, on the Essex coast, was originally a small Saxon
settlement, a natural foothold for invaders from the Continent. As a
result of royal patronage in the early nineteenth century, it slowly grew
in popularity as a resort. By 1860 it was still a small town, but the
coming of the railway and steam-powered ferries from London
transformed the area. In this century it has mushroomed as a commuter
town for Londoners, and now has a population in excess of 175,000.

On the left of the picture is the world's longest pleasure pier,
stretching for one and a quarter miles. During the Second World War it
was renamed HMS *Leigh* and used as a control centre for all Thames
shipping. 3,000 convoy conferences were held there, and over 84,000
ships sailed in convoys from Southend. The present form of the pier
originated a hundred years ago, but before that there existed a structure
with parts dating from 1825 and even earlier, described as a 'wooden
sea-serpent centipede', which was purchased by the Southend Local
Board in 1875. In its long history the pier has suffered the onslaught of
storms, and been hit by ships nine times. The most dramatic and
damaging event was the fire of 1976, the pier trains being used to
evacuate 500 trippers. Fire tugs pumped water at the rate of 50,000
gallons per minute, a torrent heroically augmented by a crop-spraying
plane, which dropped water as it flew through the flames at low level.
The last word goes to Sir John Betjeman: 'The Pier is Southend,
Southend is the Pier.'

← **114. Whitstable, Kent**

The houses in the triangular area in the centre of this picture are fishermen's residences dating from the time when Whitstable was an important fishing port. The town is still famous for its oyster-beds, but like other small fishing ports its importance has declined. The harbour, once full of working boats, is now an offloading point for sand and gravel, which are recovered locally and shipped for the manufacture of concrete.

115. Thames Ditton Island, Surrey

The Thames has a number of islands between its banks, and most have remained uninhabited. Thames Ditton Island is one of the exceptions; here we can see a number of compact residences of post-war construction.

135

116. Abingdon, Oxon.

These new houses, completed in 1987, are an interesting example of how to harmonize a new development with its surroundings.

117. Thamesmead →

This housing project was conceived in the mid-1960s as an overspill town for London. At that time high-rise buildings were very much in fashion. Although Thamesmead is landscaped with water, this type of construction remains unpopular. The later development in the area, visible in the background, has returned to low-rise, brick-built housing.

118 & 119. Belvedere and Isle of Grain power-stations

The requirement for the water cooling of power-stations leads to them being built next to water. In the Greater London conurbation, 80 per cent of stations are positioned on the shoreline of the Thames. Belvedere power-station (first picture) is one of these, on the south bank and just downstream of Barking.

The oil-burning Isle of Grain power-station, at the mouth of the Medway, is the largest of its type in Europe, and its four 660-megawatt generators (supplemented by five 29-megawatt gas turbines for independent starting and 'peak topping-up') deliver electrical power equivalent to the total needs of Birmingham, Manchester, and Liverpool.

Both the Belvedere and Isle of Grain stations are fitted with oil-fired turbines. The Isle of Grain station is particularly massive: its main chimney, which has a base diameter of 131 feet and is 800 feet high, is a clear landmark in the flat country along this stretch of the river.

120. Northfleet cement works

Lying on the Kent coast of the Thames estuary, the Northfleet cement works are the largest in Britain, with a manufacturing capacity of almost three million tonnes per year. A cement works was first established here in 1847 by William Aspdin, the son of the inventor of Portland cement. The industry was developed along this stretch of the river because of the ready availability of clay and chalk, essential ingredients in the manufacture of cement.

We have seen that the changes in the natural environment and the river's social, economic, political, military, and cultural development have all been closely interwoven in the broadloom of history. The pleasure to be gained from the river is also merged in the tapestry, from the experience of early settlers to that of modern visitors. Alongside the predilection to build defensive structures with commanding prospects, in more settled times people of privilege lived in great riverside houses with rewarding views—the Roman villas at Hambleden, for example, and elsewhere along the course of the Thames; Hampton Court Palace and Cliveden House provide later examples.

From earliest times an eye for beauty—if we interpret correctly the armorial bearings and jewellery in burial sites—must have been part of the motivation to enjoy the riverside as a change from the great forests which covered much of the land. Allowing that the forests have been largely replaced by ordered farmland and mushrooming conurbations, the motivation is still there, as witness the growth of riverside housing in places like Temple Mill Island, Abingdon, and projected developments such as Barking Reach. The houseboats at Taggs Island, and the barges converted into living units at prestigious Little Venice on the North London orbital section of the Grand Union Canal, enjoy even closer communion with the river. The new settlements are governed by patterns of surface transport, springing up where there is easy commuter access or, in the case of Little Venice, because transport within London is becoming strangulated. In all

Chapter 7
Enjoying the River

We agree that we are overworked, and need a rest—A week on the rolling deep?—George suggests the river

JEROME K. JEROME, *Three Men in a Boat*

cases, no doubt, the pressures of commerce and industry on land prices are encouraging the growth of different life-styles.

The Thames has inspired both art and literature. The illustrations in this chapter include Mapledurham House, the inspiration for *The Forsyte Saga* and *The Wind in the Willows*. Constable was inspired by the lush green setting of Hadleigh Castle, Turner by the view from Battersea Church and by Brunel's railway bridge at Maidenhead, immortalized in his famous painting *Rain, Steam and Speed*. The location of the Tate Gallery is no accident: its riverside setting appealed to Sir Henry Tate, whose inspiration was matched by his generosity in funding the construction of the building and its initial collection of British paintings.

The Thames can boast great natural beauty as well. The upland glades near the source, the water meadows and chalkways of the middle Thames, and areas of estuarine marshland are still there, although not in their old abundance. These habitats have indigenous wildlife, and the river itself, thanks to conservation measures, again attracts and nurtures its natural stock of fish. Reservoirs and areas of coppice and marsh, free of trippers even in the Greater London area, invite the settlement of fen-type communities—the herons of Walthamstow are a good example. Special efforts have produced special domains, such as the Child-Beale Wildlife Park, the Windsor Safari Park, and Kew Gardens. These places are served by boat schedules on routes upstream from London, while downstream offerings include both old and new sights, such as Greenwich and the Thames Barrier.

Sporting activities on the river have accelerated to a level beyond the dreams of the early days of the Henley Regatta. The annual Boat Race, rowed between crews from Oxford and Cambridge Universities, has moved downriver from its initial setting at Henley (first to Westminster, and then to the present stretch between Putney and Mortlake). The Thames at London has attracted the headquarters of rowing's Amateur Racing Association and, not unexpectedly, the Royal Thames Yacht Club, which pre-dates the Royal Yacht Squadron of Cowes by some 40 years.

For Thames travellers, pursuing both cultural and frivolous ambitions, the inner man can be well satisfied. The riparian equivalents of coaching inns—riverside pubs and hotels—are conveniently adjacent to moorings for yachtsmen and boat trippers of all kinds. There are, in addition, a number of floating restaurants. The opportunity to visit riverside establishments with historical connections is greatest in London. Samuel Pepys was a frequent diner at the Prospect of Whitby in Wapping Wall, while Captain Cook patronized The Angel, on the opposite bank at Rotherhithe. The Anchor, with its minstrel's gallery, is not far from the Globe Theatre in Bankside, and had a dubious reputation in Shakespeare's day.

A boat is not essential for the appreciation of the Thames as a historical river. The Historic Ship Collection, managed by the Maritime Trust, an organization with aims parallel to those of the National Trust, offers the view of famous ships moored in the Thames. The overhead pedestrian walkway of Tower Bridge, the maze at Hampton Court Palace, and the grave of Captain Jones, master of the *Mayflower*, in the churchyard of St Mary's at Rotherhithe are all equally accessible. Among the variety of walks one could mention are the 180-mile trek, from the source to the Thames Barrier, which is being created by the Countryside Commission, and the 140-mile Saxon Shore Way.

The Thames is a treasure house to explore, and one of the greatest enjoyments has been to fly over it, to view its history from a new perspective, and to share some of that experience in the brief compass of this book.

We have had a pleasant trip, and my hearty thanks for it to old Father Thames—but I think we did well to chuck it when we did.

Three Men in a Boat

121. Wargrave, Berks.

This former medieval settlement
has a main street with some
timber-framed and Georgian
houses. As a human settlement it
probably dates from the Saxon
period: certainly the earliest
phases of the present church date
from that time. Restored in the
Victorian era, the church was
burnt down in 1914, allegedly by
members of the suffragette
movement. The founder of
London's famous waxworks,
Madame Tussaud (1760–1850), is
buried in the churchyard.

122. Medmenham Abbey, Bucks.

The original abbey, of which no
visible trace remains, was founded
in 1204 by Isabel de Bolebee,
whose father-in-law held the
manor at the time of the
Domesday survey. The ruins
visible in this photograph are
comparatively recent: they
represent an eighteenth-century
structure, though it did contain
some of the earlier material. The
house is partly late Elizabethan,
with some eighteenth-century
additions. It was used in the
mid-eighteenth century by Sir
Francis Dashwood for meetings of
his notorious Hell Fire Club.

145

123. Lechlade, Glos.

To appreciate the style of riverside settlement prior to the urbanization which characterizes most of the lower Thames, a trip up-river is appropriate. Lechlade, in the upper Thames Valley, is one of the few sites on the river that looks more impressive at ground level, with a view of the church spire rising above the willow trees and water-meadows. Nevertheless, the aerial photograph provides an interesting view of the medieval market town, where the houses are mostly constructed of local Cotswold limestone, including the roofing tiles. The church, which dominates the town, dates from 1470; it was built from the profits of the local wool trade.

124. Runnymede, Surrey

The flat area on the right of the river is the place where the Magna Carta, that famous Bill of Rights, was grudgingly approved by King John on 15 June 1215. The spirit of that occasion is reflected in more than one monument. Apart from the Magna Carta monument itself—dating only from 1957, a simple pillar of English granite erected by the American Bar Association in celebration of 'freedom under law'—there is the Kennedy Monument in Portland Stone, which links the ideals of the English-speaking world, and the Commonwealth Air Forces Memorial, recording the names of 20,455 airmen killed in action with no known grave.

The area was the site of Egham racecourse in the eighteenth and nineteenth centuries. In 1931 the land was presented to the National Trust.

125. Syon House, Middx.

Syon House was originally a nunnery, founded by Henry V in 1415. It was dissolved by Henry VIII, whose fifth wife, Catherine Howard, was imprisoned here prior to her execution. In 1547 the building then passed to the Duke of Somerset, Lord Protector of the Realm, who converted it into a great castellated mansion. Inigo Jones is believed to have made some alterations during the seventeenth century, but it was the architect Robert Adam who transformed the house, indulging his own taste for Roman classicism. Rare trees were planted in the gardens by the third Duke of Northumberland, whose adviser was William Turner (1515–68), the father of English botany. The Duke also built the Great Conservatory seen on the right.

126. Hampton Court Palace →

Hampton Court was built by Cardinal Thomas Wolsey in 1514, on land leased from the Order of St John of Jerusalem. It is sometimes presented as an example of an early 'pre-fab' building, in that the wooden parts (and they are quite extensive) were constructed near Sonning from local wood, consuming the labour of 1,000 men over nine months, and then shipped by barge down the river to the building site.

Wolsey had a rapid rise to power, becoming one of the wealthiest people in the country, but in 1529, having incurred the displeasure of Henry VIII, he was obliged to donate the palace to the king in a desperate attempt to regain royal favour. Having been pardoned, Wolsey retired to York, but the following year he was arrested on a charge of high treason and died *en route* to London. Henry VIII then set about enlarging Hampton Court, making it one of the most luxurious palaces in the kingdom. By the time of William III, 200 years later, the palace was in need of considerable modernization. Christopher Wren submitted several schemes. One of them, which fortunately was not adopted, involved the demolition of all the buildings except the Great Hall. Work on Wren's revised design started in 1689 and one of the courtyards was demolished to make way for the new Fountain Court (top right in this photograph). Wren used brick with Portland Stone embellishments, and his work can be clearly distinguished from the earlier Tudor brickwork on the left. The grounds in the top of the picture were landscaped by Capability Brown. After the death of George II in 1760 Hampton Court ceased to be occupied by a reigning monarch, and in the reign of Queen Victoria the palace was first opened to the public.

127. Ham House

Situated only 200 yards from the Thames, this splendid building at Richmond, Surrey, is one of the largest Stuart houses in the country. Built in 1610, in the reign of James I, by Sir Thomas Vavasour, it was later owned by William Murray, who was created Earl of Dysart by Charles I. This photograph views Ham House from the south, showing the seventeenth-century formal garden. Since 1948 the house has been held by the National Trust and is open to the public. Its internal decoration and furnishings closely match those enjoyed by the Duke and Duchess of Lauderdale in the late seventeenth century.

128. Fawley Court, Henley, Oxon.

A fine example of a riverside country house. Designed by Sir Christopher Wren, the house was built in 1684; the decoration of the interior is by Grinling Gibbons, supplemented by James Wyatt in 1771. The grounds were laid out by Capability Brown in 1770. Today the building serves as a college for religious studies, and it houses a museum illustrating aspects of the history of Poland.

129. Blenheim Palace

Just north of the river at Woodstock in Oxfordshire lies the only non-royal mansion to be called a palace. Situated in a vast park landscaped by Capability Brown, Blenheim Palace was given to John Churchill, Duke of Marlborough, by a grateful Queen Anne following his victory in the battle of Blenheim in 1704.

Sir John Vanbrugh was appointed architect, and the foundation-stone was laid in 1705. Churchill's wife, Sarah, quarrelled with Vanbrugh over the construction and subsequently dismissed him. The palace was completed by Hawksmoor in the 1720s. The house and parkland are open to the public. In this aerial view, taken from the south-west, the beauty of the scene is readily appreciated.

130. Cliveden

Cliveden House, just north of Maidenhead, is the third house to be built on this flat hilltop overlooking the Thames. Erected in 1851 in the classical style by Sir Charles Barry (chief architect of the Houses of Parliament) for the Duke of Sutherland, it is an impressive building, skilfully fitted into the terraces of the previous building, which was burnt down. The grounds were landscaped by Capability Brown. The Astors owned the property from 1893, and after the First World War a number of politicians and others were entertained here, becoming known as the 'Cliveden Set'. Lady Astor was the first woman to enter Parliament. The property is now owned by the National Trust, and the extensive grounds are open to the public, although the house is largely used as a prestige hotel.

← 131. Taggs Island

Taggs Island, just upstream from Hampton Court, is surrounded by houseboats. Some of the boats are converted barges; others have hulls made of concrete. One is actually a military artefact, being a pierhead pontoon from the famous Mulberry Harbour used to supply the Allied beach-head in France during the Second World War.

132. Mapledurham House

Mapledurham is a brick-built Tudor mansion constructed for the Blount family at about the time of the Spanish Armada (1588). The nearby Church of St Margaret dates mainly from the fourteenth and fifteenth centuries. Built on the site of an earlier building, it contains a number of tombs of the Blount family. The house was used by novelist John Galsworthy as one of his settings for *The Forsyte Saga*, and also provided Kenneth Grahame with the inspiration for Toad Hall in his novel *The Wind in the Willows*, written when he lived at nearby Pangbourne.

133. Bisham Abbey

Bisham Abbey, in Berkshire, dates from the fourteenth century, though its use as an abbey was discontinued in the time of Henry VIII. Some of the structure of the abbey has been incorporated in a recreational complex for the National Sports Council, the building in the centre of the picture being part of the National Tennis Centre, which has one of the world's largest areas of artificial grass.

134. Bisham Church

Bisham Church of All Saints has retained its twelfth-century tower, although the rest of the building was heavily restored in the nineteenth century. It contains some fine Elizabethan tombs of the Hoby family.

135. Tate Gallery

The art gallery at Millbank, facing the London Thames, was founded by Sir Henry Tate, the sugar refiner, and opened in 1897. Built by Sidney Smith in the classical style, it houses a fine collection of modern art, as well as British art from all periods. Sir Henry's gift of seventy British paintings formed the nucleus of the collection. Extensions were built in the period 1899–1906, also at his expense, and there have been further additions later in this century. The Clore Gallery containing the Turner Collection opened in 1987.

136. Child-Beale Wildlife Trust →

The path of the Thames passes through the Goring Gap, at the southern extremity of the Chiltern Hills. In the foreground is the Child-Beale Wildlife Trust, founded in 1956 by Gilbert Ernest Child-Beale, a founder shareholder of Carters Seeds, to be enjoyed in memory of his parents. The statues which adorn the grounds were collected from places throughout England. The Beale Bird Park is an important part of the Trust, and its river entrance is served by a pleasant six-mile boat trip from the centre of Reading, or as part of the itinerary offered by pleasure cruises from London.

137. Palm House, Kew Gardens

Kew Gardens were started in 1759 as a hobby of Princess Augusta, the mother of George III. The botanical collections took off under Sir Joseph Banks, who dispatched botanists to Africa, Asia, and the Pacific Islands in search of exotic species. Banks, who became President of the Royal Society, was a great traveller himself, and left his name in distant places, including Banks Island in the Canadian Arctic and Bankstown, a suburb of Sydney, Australia, overlooking Botany Bay. Queen Victoria presented Kew Gardens to the nation in 1840. Unfortunately a number of trees fell victim to the Great Storm of October 1987.

The Palm House, restored in the 1980s, contains an impressive variety of palms. It was built in 1844–8 to the design of Decimus Burton, and for many years was the largest glasshouse in the world: 362 feet long and 66 feet high, with over 45,000 square feet of glass. The iron frame was prefabricated by Richard Turner at his ironworks in Dublin. The structure is part of a grand Victorian tradition of buildings in iron and glass, including the Crystal Palace (since destroyed) and a number of railway stations.

138. Margate

Originally known as 'Bartholomew Fair by the Sea', Margate was a small fishing port before becoming a fashionable Victorian seaside resort. Its popularity began to rise with the introduction of the 'Saturday Boat', which brought Londoners down the river for a day or weekend by the sea. In 1812 Margate received 17,000 visitors, mostly from London, and by 1856 the figure had risen to 105,000.

Some Victorian terrace-houses can be seen in the centre of this picture. It was at Margate that sea bathing first became popular, and bathing-machines made their début on this beach.

← 139. The Henley Regatta

Henley during the annual Regatta, held in the first week of July. The Regatta was first held in 1839, becoming the Royal Regatta with the patronage of Prince Albert in 1851. The first Oxford and Cambridge Boat Race was rowed between Hambleden and Henley in 1829.

140. Yachting at Cookham, Berks.

163

141. Boveney Lock

The next lock upstream from Windsor. A lock at this point was first mentioned in a lease dated 1535. A pound-lock was built in 1838, and in 1871 the Thames Conservancy agreed that the boys of the nearby Eton College could use the lock for their boats: the agreed sum for that concession was £35 per annum, but by 1916 this had risen to £60. The lock shown in this picture is the product of rebuilding in 1898.

142. Thorpe Park

In Surrey near Heathrow Airport, Thorpe Park is a large 'theme park', situated in a series of abandoned gravel pits adjacent to the river. It was set up at considerable expense by a company that had previously worked the pits to extract gravel for the manufacture of building materials. It can be seen as a public relations exercise to show the amenity value of disused gravel pits as areas for nature reserves and recreational facilities. The original intention was to illustrate the history of Britain on land, sea, and air. There are reconstructions of castles, Roman villas, and other buildings from the past. At one time it displayed a spectacular collection of flying replicas of famous aircraft, including the precursor of the Spitfire, the Supermarine S6B float-plane, which won the Schneider Trophy race in 1931. Sadly, most of the aircraft collection has been sold off in recent years. Among the ships are replicas of a Roman galleon and a Viking long ship.

← 143. Eel Pie Island

Eel Pie Island, by Twickenham, was a favourite picnic spot in Edwardian times. The island acquired its name because visitors to a hotel, since demolished, relished its speciality of eels and lampreys for Sunday tea.

144. Evening on the Thames

The river is now being used much more for recreational purposes. Here a launch heads up-river from Medmenham in Buckinghamshire on a hot summer evening.

145. *Old Father Thames*

This statue was created out of Portland cement concrete by the famous Victorian sculptor Rafaelle Monti for the Great Exhibition of 1851. It is an interesting early use of what has become one of the world's foremost building materials.

The statue survived the Crystal Palace fire of 1936, and in 1958 it was set up close to the official source of the river at Thameshead. Unfortunately, in its Thameshead location it was vandalized. Restored, it was resited in its present position at St John's Lock (Plate 105), by Lechlade, Gloucestershire, in 1974.

Index